This work is dedicated in memory of each of our fathers:

RABBI DR. BARRET BROYDE
LARRY B. TRAVIS

And in honor of our mothers, may they each live long and prosper:

DR. SUSE BROYDE
INA R. TRAVIS

If there is a deep and important theme to the book of Genesis, the idea that parents impact how their children turn out is a major one, and we were both blessed to be raised by loving, caring parents. As we age, we appreciate our parents very much, miss our fathers intensely, and hope we are parents and grandparents as good as our own parents were.

SEX IN THE GARDEN

SEX IN THE GARDEN

Consensual Encounters Gone Bad

Michael J. Broyde

and

Reuven Travis

WIPF & STOCK · Eugene, Oregon

SEX IN THE GARDEN
Consensual Encounters Gone Bad

Wipf & Stock
An Imprint of Wipf and Stock Publishers
199 W. 8th Ave., Suite 3
Eugene, OR 97401

www.wipfandstock.com

PAPERBACK ISBN: 978-1-5326-8437-1
HARDCOVER ISBN: 978-1-5326-8438-8
EBOOK ISBN: 978-1-5326-8439-5

Manufactured in the U.S.A.   JULY 2, 2019

Contents

About the Authors

Michael J. Broyde

RABBI BROYDE is Professor of Law at Emory University School of Law and a Senior Fellow at the Center for the Study of Law and Religion at Emory University. His primary areas of interest are law and religion, Jewish law and ethics, and comparative religious law. Besides Jewish law and family law, Rabbi Broyde has taught Federal Courts, Alternative Dispute Resolution, and Secured Credit and Bankruptcy. He received a *juris doctor* from New York University and published a note on the law review. He clerked for Judge Leonard I. Garth of the United States Court of Appeals for the Third Circuit. Most recently, in 2018, Rabbi Broyde won a Fulbright Senior Scholar Fellowship to study religious arbitration in diverse western democracies. In 2019, he will be visiting at Stanford Law School, teaching Jewish Law.

Rabbi Broyde is ordained as a rabbi by Yeshiva University and was a member of the Beth Din of America, the largest Jewish law court in America. He was the director of that court during the 1997–1998 academic year while on leave from Emory. Rabbi Broyde was also the founding rabbi of the Young Israel synagogue in Atlanta, where he served for many years as the rabbi, a founder of the Atlanta Torah MiTzion Kollel study program, and a board member of many organizations in Atlanta.

Reuven Travis

RABBI TRAVIS spent fifteen years as an advertising and marketing executive working for large Fortune 500 firms such as Georgia-Pacific and Ogilvy & Mather and as a consultant. He developed strategic business and marketing plans for a variety of consumer packaged goods and financial services companies. Twenty years ago, Rabbi Travis changed professions and started his career as an educator. In that time, he has taught a wide range of classes, including Jewish law, Bible, Jewish history, Zionism and the Shoah, Israel advocacy, American history and civics, and African-American history.

Rabbi Travis earned his bachelor's degree from Dartmouth College, where he graduated Phi Beta Kappa, with a double major in French literature and political science. He holds a master's degree in teaching from Mercer University and also earned a master's in Judaic studies from Spertus College. He received his rabbinic ordination in 2006 from Rabbi Michael J. Broyde, dean of the Atlanta Torah MiTzion Kollel, after spending four years studying with Rabbi Broyde and the members of the kollel.

Rabbi Travis has previously published studies of the book of Job (*From Job to the Shoah: A Story of Dust and Ashes*) and the book of Numbers (*Sefer BeMidbar as Sefer HaMiddot: The Book of Numbers as the Book of Character Development*).

Preface

THE HEBREW BIBLE SERVES many different purposes in the Western Canon. A few readily come to mind.

The Hebrew Bible is a law book for those traditionally observant of Jewish law (as both of us are). We eat only the animals labeled kosher in Leviticus; we faithfully observe the Sabbath as described in many places; we celebrate the biblical festivals, and so on. *We did not write this book for the community that sees the Hebrew Bible as a law book. There is very little focus on technical Jewish law here, and ours is hardly a law book.*

The Hebrew Bible is also a history book for the Land of Israel in premodern times. Anyone who has toured Israel encounters artifacts and monuments (real and fake) to stories from the Hebrew Bible. *We did not write this book for the history-oriented community. Archaeology is hardly our focus, and the details of biblical history are of little interest to us in our analysis of Genesis.*

The Hebrew Bible is a precursor to the New Testament for many Christians, setting the table for the stories found therein. *This book certainly does not examine the stories or laws of the Hebrew Bible in light of the New Testament.*

The Hebrew Bible is a literary magnum opus in ancient Hebrew. *From a literary perspective, we are not parsing the details of Hebrew grammar in this book, as fascinating a question as this seems to some.*

So, what is the purpose of this book? As one of the oldest books in constant use, the Hebrew Bible has stories and tales that have been told over many times to adults and children. It contains several morality tales that apply to society, from the story of Moses's woes as a leader, to David's triumph over Goliath, and so much more. The Bible tells us stories that inspire and direct us. To put it differently, most people who pick up the Bible do so because they are interested in understanding how the biblical message can impact them and help them with the complexities of their life, and not because they aspire to be a scholar of Hebrew grammar or an archeologist of biblical lands. Rather, the Bible is the best and most important self-help book ever written, and its stories are designed to inspire values and virtues needed to make every person successful, important, moral, and just.

This book focuses on the deeper messages of the stories of Genesis that apply to a modern American society, which has mostly discarded the historical ethic on family matters shared by Judaism and Christianity, from adultery to divorce and onward. The highest court in New York framed the basic model of American sexual ethics in a case named *People v. Ronald Onofre*. The court ruled that all sexual activity people engage in is legal so long as they are "voluntarily made by adults in a noncommercial private setting." Per this ruling, these sexual activities are protected by the right to privacy. Not so in the Jewish tradition. By the time the Jewish people finish receiving the Torah, there is clearly more to sexual ethics than the four ideas of (1) voluntarily made by (2) adults in a (3) noncommercial (4) private setting.

Ours is a reread of the book of Genesis which focuses on the sexual ethics component of the Genesis narrative. It is not for scholars of Hebrew grammar or people deeply interested in Jewish law (*halakhah*), nor is it a precursor to the New Testament. Rather, ours is an attempt to read the whole book of Genesis as a tale of sexual morality. We see Genesis as preaching against leaving the limits of human sexuality to consent and privacy, adulthood, or noncommercial matters. Moreover, we believe Genesis does so by showing what happens to individuals and society when limits are set in this manner.

Needless to say, we hope that this book causes readers to reflect on modern America in a certain way and impacts the choices people make in their own lives and families.

A Brief Note on the Intellectual History of this Work

This book started as a series of lectures in the Young Israel of Toco Hills almost twenty years ago when one of us (MJB) was the rabbi there. These lectures were transcribed by Jennifer Harris, then executive director of the Young Israel and now of Emory University, and the initial manuscript was reedited by Sara Miller, who resides in Israel. The project then languished unfinished for many years until one of us (RT) undertook to substantially expand the thrust of this work and turn it into a self-standing and thoughtful commentary geared to a community markedly broader than the original synagogue audience it was first written for.

We are grateful to the many people who helped us turn this into the excellent work it is. Thank you to all of you. There are many to list, but we particularly want to thank Rabbi Dr. Michael Berger and Rabbi Dr. Don Seeman for their feedback and insights. Thanks also to Ms. Lisa Marks and Ms. Rachel Travis, who were important sounding boards as the written words to this book were taking shape.

Michael J. Broyde
Reuven Travis

CHAPTER 1

Introduction and Selected Excerpts from the Book of Genesis

LET US START WITH an observation that does not seem at all obvious until it is articulated. Only when it is stated outright do people wonder how they overlooked it.

The book of Genesis contains no laws. God gives no "thou shalt" or "thou shall not" commandments to humanity. Instead, the figures in Genesis operate based on personal choice and personal freedom, especially when it comes to interpersonal relations. Yes, there were social mores at work, as when Laban tells Jacob: "It is not the practice in our place to marry off the younger before the older" (Genesis 29:26). But there were no courts or judges who would supervise and enforce this practice. People were free to do as they chose when it came to matters of sex and marriage, just as it fell to them to deal with the consequences of their decisions for their lovers, spouses, or families.

If you think this sounds quite a bit like life in America in the twenty-first century, we would agree, and that is why we've written this book.

People today seem less inclined to study the Bible in general and Genesis in particular. Scientific theories such as the Big Bang and evolution are routinely taught in our public schools, which calls the validity of the Gospels (and of the Pentateuch) into question in the minds of many individuals. In other words, they think, "What does Genesis have to do with our lives? What of relevance could it possibly teach us?"

Quite a bit actually, as we hope to demonstrate throughout this book.

There is another reason we believe people shy away from reading Genesis as adults. They think they already know its stories and what morals it has to teach. This is not surprising. People of all Abrahamic faiths—Jews, Christians, Muslims—frequently learn Genesis in-depth as children, be it at home, during worship services, or in a formal education setting such as a Sunday school or full-time parochial school.

Why Genesis and not any of the Pentateuch's other four books? Genesis is full of tales that children can appreciate: stories of good and bad characters, stories of God dealing directly with the world, stories about families. These are precisely the types of stories children can relate to and can learn with relative ease, particularly compared to the book of Leviticus, with its emphasis on the sacrificial rites in the Tabernacle or the book of Numbers, with its many stories of a wrathful God wreaking havoc upon the Jews in the wilderness for the various sins they commit. Having learned Genesis as children, people may ask, "Why learn it again?"

For us, this is an unfortunate situation.

The situations in the many stories of Genesis echo the way people approach matters of sex and marriage in modern America. Genesis does not come to preach—remember its lack of "thou shalts" and "thou shalt nots." It comes to teach that lawful or culturally acceptable relationships entered into freely by all parties can nonetheless have very real and very serious effects on people's lives.[1] This is why we believe it so important that adults of all denominations revisit the book of Genesis with an open mind and

1. We acknowledge that the notion of entering freely into an arrangement or of consent has a very different meaning today than it did in in ancient Israel, especially for women. Were this a historical as opposed to a literary study, we would explore these differences at length. For our purposes, when we use the terms "consent" or "consensual," we do so with their simplest meaning, apart from the historical and even contemporary baggage that complicates the issue.

with an adult perspective. Said differently, what readers of Genesis can learn from the relational dynamics in its stories will prove helpful today, even though these stories are built upon a very different culture with regard to sexuality.

This is more difficult than one might think.

Let's assume that, in the pages that follow, we successfully make the case to adults for relearning Genesis (and not merely rereading its stories). It is actually difficult for most people who might have studied it as children to set aside the storybook versions of the tales they were taught and come to see the book with a more realistic and more adult perspective.

This is not speculation on our part. This is based on research.

There are accepted pedagogical reasons why unlearning something and then relearning it is hard, and these center on the role of prior knowledge as it relates to learning. One of the ways in which unlearning occurs comes through a process of extinction or "the removal of reinforcements."[2] Our experience has shown this to be very much the case. We both have seen people encounter memorable Bible stories as children, develop a certain understanding of Genesis based on them, and then find it difficult to relearn the book in a more multifaceted and adult manner.

As rabbis and teachers, we encounter this phenomenon frequently. We know that a deeper, more nuanced understanding of the Bible comes later in a person's educational development, when critical thinking skills and maturity reach a level that enables a person to fully engage with the biblical narrative. Yet, when it comes to Genesis, because so many of our students studied the book relatively intensely as children, they find it fundamentally difficult to see important themes in the book when revisiting it as adults.

Here is but one example: Sexuality is a dominant theme of the book of Genesis that educators consciously avoid when teaching children. It permeates the entire book, from the discovery of human sexuality in the garden of Eden, to the sexual and emotional tension between Rachel and Leah, to the complicated sexual

2. Lee, "Unlearning," para. 2.

encounter between Judah and Tamar, to the wife of Potiphar's open lust for Joseph. For obvious reasons, teachers choose to ignore all of these when Genesis is taught in elementary schools. They instead focus on simpler stories, such as the animals coming two by two into Noah's ark, the three angels visiting Abraham, or Rebekah running to the well to water Eliezer's camels. These simpler stories set forth important lessons for children about being hospitable and caring for others. In contrast, the sexual stories raise too many questions that are unintelligible for children to ask and almost impossible for teachers to answer.

The way in which people encounter the book of Genesis as children thus leaves them with a diminished or possibly with even no understanding of its treatment of sexuality or of the other complex themes set forth in this foundational book. Yet it is precisely this full and adult understanding of Genesis we believe can be so relevant to and so important for our times.

Our goal in writing this book is to reintroduce adults to the various storylines of Genesis, with all their complexities and to challenge our readers to unlearn the book in order to relearn it. When they do, they will see that Genesis is a narrative composed of many rich themes that resonate in important ways for modern readers.

The Genesis Stories (Chapter and Verse)

Some readers of this book are likely familiar with the Genesis stories we examine in the chapters that follow. Others may never have read either the chapters or the verses of these stories. Yet even one with the most cursory knowledge of the Bible will be able to follow our presentation and analysis of the best-known storylines in Genesis. All the same, we thought it worthwhile to set forth here the stories that are at the heart of this book, and we have done so in the order in which they appear in Genesis, not the order in which we deal with each in our study.

There are many fine translations of the Bible in general, and of Genesis in particular. We have opted to use *Tanakh: A New*

Translation of the Holy Scriptures according to the Traditional Hebrew Text (Philadelphia, PA: Jewish Publication Society of America, 1985) unless otherwise indicated. This translation is available via Sefaria (www.sefaria.org), a non-profit organization dedicated to assembling a free living library of Jewish texts, with the goal, in their own words, "of making all the books of the Bible available to the public."

Adam and Eve (Genesis 1:26—3:24)

And God said, "Let us make man in our image, after our likeness. They shall rule the fish of the sea, the birds of the sky, the cattle, the whole earth, and all the creeping things that creep on earth." And God created man in His image, in the image of God He created him; male and female He created them. God blessed them and God said to them, "Be fertile and increase, fill the earth and master it; and rule the fish of the sea, the birds of the sky, and all the living things that creep on earth."

God said, "See, I give you every seed-bearing plant that is upon all the earth, and every tree that has seed-bearing fruit; they shall be yours for food. And to all the animals on land, to all the birds of the sky, and to everything that creeps on earth, in which there is the breath of life, [I give] all the green plants for food." And it was so. And God saw all that He had made, and found it very good. And there was evening and there was morning, the sixth day.

The heaven and the earth were finished, and all their array. On the seventh day God finished the work that He had been doing, and He ceased on the seventh day from all the work that He had done. And God blessed the seventh day and declared it holy, because on it God ceased from all the work of creation that He had done. Such is the story of heaven and earth when they were created.

§

When the Lord God made earth and heaven—when no shrub of the field was yet on earth and no grasses of the field had yet sprouted, because the Lord God had not sent rain upon the earth and there was no man to till the soil, but a flow would well up from the ground and water the whole surface of the earth—the Lord God formed man from the dust of the earth. He blew into his nostrils the breath of life, and man became a living being.

The Lord God planted a garden in Eden, in the east, and placed there the man whom He had formed. And from the ground the Lord God caused to grow every tree that was pleasing to the sight and good for food, with the tree of life in the middle of the garden, and the tree of knowledge of good and bad.

A river issues from Eden to water the garden, and it then divides and becomes four branches. The name of the first is Pishon, the one that winds through the whole land of Havilah, where the gold is. (The gold of that land is good; bdellium is there, and lapis lazuli.) The name of the second river is Gihon, the one that winds through the whole land of Cush. The name of the third river is Tigris, the one that flows east of Asshur. And the fourth river is the Euphrates.

The Lord God took the man and placed him in the Garden of Eden, to till it and tend it. And the Lord God commanded the man, saying, "Of every tree of the garden you are free to eat; but as for the tree of knowledge of good and bad, you must not eat of it; for as soon as you eat of it, you shall die."

The Lord God said, "It is not good for man to be alone; I will make a fitting helper for him." And the Lord God formed out of the earth all the wild beasts and all the birds of the sky, and brought them to the man to see what he would call them; and whatever the man called each living creature, that would be its name. And the man gave names to all the cattle and to the birds of the sky and to all the wild beasts; but for Adam no fitting helper was found. So the Lord God cast a deep sleep upon the man; and, while he slept, He took one of his ribs and closed up the flesh at that spot. And the Lord God fashioned the rib that He had taken from the man into a woman; and He brought her to the man. Then the man said,

> "This one at last
> Is bone of my bones
> And flesh of my flesh.
> This one shall be called Woman,
> For from man was she taken."

Hence a man leaves his father and mother and clings to his wife, so that they become one flesh.

The two of them were naked, the man and his wife, yet they felt no shame. Now the serpent was the shrewdest of all the wild beasts that the Lord God had made. He said to the woman, "Did God really say: You shall not eat of any tree of the garden?" The woman replied to the serpent, "We may eat of the fruit of the other trees of the garden. It is only about fruit of the tree in the middle of the garden that God said: 'You shall not eat of it or touch it, lest you die.'" And the serpent said to the woman, "You are not going to die, but God knows that as soon as you eat of it your eyes will be opened and you will be like divine beings who know good and bad." When the woman saw that the tree was good for eating and a delight to the eyes, and that the tree was desirable as a source of wisdom, she took of its fruit and ate. She also gave some to her husband, and he ate. Then the eyes of both of them were opened and they perceived that they were naked; and they sewed together fig leaves and made themselves loincloths.

They heard the sound of the Lord God moving about in the garden at the breezy time of day; and the man and his wife hid from the Lord God among the trees of the garden. The Lord God called out to the man and said to him, "Where are you?" He replied, "I heard the sound of You in the garden, and I was afraid because I was naked, so I hid." Then He asked, "Who told you that you were naked? Did you eat of the tree from which I had forbidden you to eat?" The man said, "The woman You put at my side—she gave me of the tree, and I ate." And the Lord God said to the woman, "What is this you have done!" The woman replied, "The serpent duped me, and I ate." Then the Lord God said to the serpent,

> "Because you did this,
> More cursed shall you be
> Than all cattle
> And all the wild beasts:
> On your belly shall you crawl
> And dirt shall you eat
> All the days of your life.
> I will put enmity
> Between you and the woman,
> And between your offspring and hers;
> They shall strike at your head,
> And you shall strike at their heel."

And to the woman He said,

> "I will make most severe
> Your pangs in childbearing;
> In pain shall you bear children.
> Yet your urge shall be for your husband,
> And he shall rule over you."

To Adam He said, "Because you did as your wife said and ate of the tree about which I commanded you, 'You shall not eat of it,'

> Cursed be the ground because of you;
> By toil shall you eat of it
> All the days of your life:
> Thorns and thistles shall it sprout for you.
> But your food shall be the grasses of the field;
> by the sweat of your brow shall you get bread to eat,
> Until you return to the ground—
> For from it you were taken.

For dust you are,
And to dust you shall return."

The man named his wife Eve, because she was the mother of all the living. And the Lord God made garments of skins for Adam and his wife, and clothed them.

And the Lord God said, "Now that the man has become like one of us, knowing good and bad, what if he should stretch out his hand and take also from the tree of life and eat, and live forever!" So the Lord God banished him from the garden of Eden, to till the soil from which he was taken. He drove the man out, and stationed east of the garden of Eden the cherubim and the fiery ever-turning sword, to guard the way to the tree of life.

Cain and Abel (Genesis 4:1–16)

Now the man knew his wife Eve, and she conceived and bore Cain, saying, "I have gained a male child with the help of the Lord." She then bore his brother Abel. Abel became a keeper of sheep, and Cain became a tiller of the soil. In the course of time, Cain brought an offering to the Lord from the fruit of the soil; and Abel, for his part, brought the choicest of the firstlings of his flock. The Lord paid heed to Abel and his offering, but to Cain and his offering He paid no heed. Cain was much distressed and his face fell. And the Lord said to Cain,

"Why are you distressed,
And why is your face fallen?
Surely, if you do right,
There is uplift.
But if you do not do right
Sin couches at the door;
Its urge is toward you,
Yet you can be its master."

Cain said to his brother Abel . . . and when they were in the field, Cain set upon his brother Abel and killed him. The Lord said to

Cain, "Where is your brother Abel?" And he said, "I do not know. Am I my brother's keeper?" Then He said, "What have you done? Hark, your brother's blood cries out to Me from the ground! Therefore, you shall be more cursed than the ground, which opened its mouth to receive your brother's blood from your hand. If you till the soil, it shall no longer yield its strength to you. You shall become a ceaseless wanderer on earth."

Cain said to the Lord, "My punishment is too great to bear! Since You have banished me this day from the soil, and I must avoid Your presence and become a restless wanderer on earth— anyone who meets me may kill me!" The Lord said to him, "I promise, if anyone kills Cain, sevenfold vengeance shall be taken on him." And the Lord put a mark on Cain, lest anyone who met him should kill him. Cain left the presence of the Lord and settled in the land of Nod, east of Eden.

Abraham and Sarah
(Genesis 12:1–20; 16:1–16; 20:1–18)

The Lord said to Abram, "Go forth from your native land and from your father's house to the land that I will show you.

> I will make of you a great nation,
> And I will bless you;
> I will make your name great,
> And you shall be a blessing.
> I will bless those who bless you
> And curse him that curses you;
> And all the families of the earth
> Shall bless themselves by you."

Abram went forth as the Lord had commanded him, and Lot went with him. Abram was seventy-five years old when he left Haran. Abram took his wife Sarai and his brother's son Lot, and all the wealth that they had amassed, and the persons that they had acquired in Haran; and they set out for the land of Canaan. When they arrived in the land of Canaan, Abram passed through the land as far as the site of Shechem, at the terebinth of Moreh. The Canaanites were then in the land.

The Lord appeared to Abram and said, "I will assign this land to your offspring." And he built an altar there to the Lord who had appeared to him. From there he moved on to the hill country east of Bethel and pitched his tent, with Bethel on the west and Ai on the east; and he built there an altar to the Lord and invoked the Lord by name. Then Abram journeyed by stages toward the Negeb.

§

There was a famine in the land, and Abram went down to Egypt to sojourn there, for the famine was severe in the land. As he was about to enter Egypt, he said to his wife Sarai, "I know what a beautiful woman you are. If the Egyptians see you, and think, 'She is his wife,' they will kill me and let you live. Please say that you are my sister, that it may go well with me because of you, and that I may remain alive thanks to you."

When Abram entered Egypt, the Egyptians saw how very beautiful the woman was. Pharaoh's courtiers saw her and praised her to Pharaoh, and the woman was taken into Pharaoh's palace. And because of her, it went well with Abram; he acquired sheep, oxen, asses, male and female slaves, she-asses, and camels.

But the Lord afflicted Pharaoh and his household with mighty plagues on account of Sarai, the wife of Abram. Pharaoh sent for Abram and said, "What is this you have done to me! Why did you not tell me that she was your wife? Why did you say, 'She is my sister,' so that I took her as my wife? Now, here is your wife; take her and begone!" And Pharaoh put men in charge of him, and they sent him off with his wife and all that he possessed.

§

Sarai, Abram's wife, had borne him no children. She had an Egyptian maidservant whose name was Hagar. And Sarai said to Abram, "Look, the Lord has kept me from bearing. Consort with my maid;

perhaps I shall have a son through her." And Abram heeded Sarai's request. So Sarai, Abram's wife, took her maid, Hagar the Egyptian—after Abram had dwelt in the land of Canaan ten years—and gave her to her husband Abram as concubine. He cohabited with Hagar and she conceived; and when she saw that she had conceived, her mistress was lowered in her esteem. And Sarai said to Abram, "The wrong done me is your fault! I myself put my maid in your bosom; now that she sees that she is pregnant, I am lowered in her esteem. The Lord decide between you and me!" Abram said to Sarai, "Your maid is in your hands. Deal with her as you think right." Then Sarai treated her harshly, and she ran away from her.

An angel of the Lord found her by a spring of water in the wilderness, the spring on the road to Shur, and said, "Hagar, slave of Sarai, where have you come from, and where are you going?" And she said, "I am running away from my mistress Sarai." And the angel of the Lord said to her, "Go back to your mistress, and submit to her harsh treatment." And the angel of the Lord said to her,

> "I will greatly increase your offspring,
> And they shall be too many to count."

The angel of the Lord said to her further,

> "Behold, you are with child
> And shall bear a son;
> You shall call him Ishmael,
> For the Lord has paid heed to your suffering.
> He shall be a wild ass of a man;
> His hand against everyone,
> And everyone's hand against him;
> He shall dwell alongside of all his kinsmen."

And she called the Lord who spoke to her, "You Are El-roi," by which she meant, "Have I not gone on seeing after He saw me!" Therefore the well was called Beer-lahai-roi; it is between Kadesh and Bered.—Hagar bore a son to Abram, and Abram gave the son that Hagar bore him the name Ishmael. Abram was eighty-six years old when Hagar bore Ishmael to Abram.

§

Abraham journeyed from there to the region of the Negeb and settled between Kadesh and Shur. While he was sojourning in Gerar, Abraham said of Sarah his wife, "She is my sister." So King Abimelech of Gerar had Sarah brought to him. But God came to Abimelech in a dream by night and said to him, "You are to die because of the woman that you have taken, for she is a married woman." Now Abimelech had not approached her. He said, "O Lord, will You slay people even though innocent? He himself said to me, 'She is my sister!' And she also said, 'He is my brother.' When I did this, my heart was blameless and my hands were clean." And God said to him in the dream, "I knew that you did this with a blameless heart, and so I kept you from sinning against Me. That was why I did not let you touch her. Therefore, restore the man's wife—since he is a prophet, he will intercede for you—to save your life. If you fail to restore her, know that you shall die, you and all that are yours."

Early next morning, Abimelech called his servants and told them all that had happened; and the men were greatly frightened. Then Abimelech summoned Abraham and said to him, "What have you done to us? What wrong have I done that you should bring so great a guilt upon me and my kingdom? You have done to me things that ought not to be done. What, then," Abimelech demanded of Abraham, "was your purpose in doing this thing?" "I thought," said Abraham, "surely there is no fear of God in this place, and they will kill me because of my wife. And besides, she is in truth my sister, my father's daughter though not my mother's; and she became my wife. So when God made me wander from my father's house, I said to her, 'Let this be the kindness that you shall do me: whatever place we come to, say there of me: He is my brother.'"

Abimelech took sheep and oxen, and male and female slaves, and gave them to Abraham; and he restored his wife Sarah to him. And Abimelech said, "Here, my land is before you; settle wherever you please." And to Sarah he said, "I herewith give your brother a thousand pieces of silver; this will serve you as vindication before all who are with you, and you are cleared before everyone." Abraham then prayed to God, and God healed Abimelech and his wife and his slave girls, so that they bore children; for the Lord had closed fast every womb of the household of Abimelech because of Sarah, the wife of Abraham.

Isaac and Rebekah
(Genesis 24:62–67; 25:19–28; 26:1–11)

Isaac had just come back from the vicinity of Beer-lahai-roi, for he was settled in the region of the Negeb. And Isaac went out walking in the field toward evening and, looking up, he saw camels approaching. Raising her eyes, Rebekah saw Isaac. She alighted from the camel and said to the servant, "Who is that man walking in the field toward us?" And the servant said, "That is my master." So she took her veil and covered herself. The servant told Isaac all the things that he had done. Isaac then brought her into the tent of his mother Sarah, and he took Rebekah as his wife. Isaac loved her, and thus found comfort after his mother's death.

This is the story of Isaac, son of Abraham. Abraham begot Isaac. Isaac was forty years old when he took to wife Rebekah, daughter of Bethuel the Aramean of Paddan-aram, sister of Laban the Aramean. Isaac pleaded with the Lord on behalf of his wife, because she was barren; and the Lord responded to his plea, and his wife Rebekah conceived. But the children struggled in her womb, and she said, "If so, why do I exist?" She went to inquire of the Lord, and the Lord answered her,

> "Two nations are in your womb,
> Two separate peoples shall issue from your body;
> One people shall be mightier than the other,
> And the older shall serve the younger."

When her time to give birth was at hand, there were twins in her womb. The first one emerged red, like a hairy mantle all over; so they named him Esau. Then his brother emerged, holding on to the heel of Esau; so they named him Jacob. Isaac was sixty years old when they were born.

When the boys grew up, Esau became a skillful hunter, a man of the outdoors; but Jacob was a mild man who stayed in camp. Isaac favored Esau because he had a taste for game; but Rebekah favored Jacob.

§

There was a famine in the land—aside from the previous famine that had occurred in the days of Abraham—and Isaac went to Abimelech, king of the Philistines, in Gerar. The Lord had appeared to him and said, "Do not go down to Egypt; stay in the land which I point out to you. Reside in this land, and I will be with you and bless you; I will assign all these lands to you and to your offspring, fulfilling the oath that I swore to your father Abraham. I will make your descendants as numerous as the stars of heaven, and give to your descendants all these lands, so that all the nations of the earth shall bless themselves by your offspring—inasmuch as Abraham obeyed Me and kept My charge: My commandments, My laws, and My teachings."

So Isaac stayed in Gerar. When the men of the place asked him about his wife, he said, "She is my sister," for he was afraid to say "my wife," thinking, "The men of the place might kill me on account of Rebekah, for she is beautiful." When some time had passed, Abimelech king of the Philistines, looking out of the window, saw Isaac fondling his wife Rebekah. Abimelech sent for Isaac and said, "So she is your wife! Why then did you say: 'She is my sister?'" Isaac said to him, "Because I thought I might lose my life on account of her." Abimelech said, "What have you done to us! One of the people might have lain with your wife, and you would have brought guilt upon us." Abimelech then charged all the people, saying, "Anyone who molests this man or his wife shall be put to death."

Jacob and Esau (Genesis 27:1–46)

When Isaac was old and his eyes were too dim to see, he called his older son Esau and said to him, "My son." He answered, "Here I am." And he said, "I am old now, and I do not know how soon I may die. Take your gear, your quiver and bow, and go out into the open and hunt me some game. Then prepare a dish for me such as I like, and bring it to me to eat, so that I may give you my innermost blessing before I die."

Rebekah had been listening as Isaac spoke to his son Esau. When Esau had gone out into the open to hunt game to bring home, Rebekah said to her son Jacob, "I overheard your father speaking to your brother Esau, saying, 'Bring me some game and prepare a dish for me to eat, that I may bless you, with the Lord's approval, before I die.' Now, my son, listen carefully as I instruct you. Go to the flock and fetch me two choice kids, and I will make of them a dish for your father, such as he likes. Then take it to your father to eat, in order that he may bless you before he dies." Jacob answered his mother Rebekah, "But my brother Esau is a hairy man and I am smooth-skinned. If my father touches me, I shall appear to him as a trickster and bring upon myself a curse, not a blessing." But his mother said to him, "Your curse, my son, be upon me! Just do as I say and go fetch them for me."

He got them and brought them to his mother, and his mother prepared a dish such as his father liked. Rebekah then took the best clothes of her older son Esau, which were there in the house, and had her younger son Jacob put them on; and she covered his hands and the hairless part of his neck with the skins of the kids. Then she put in the hands of her son Jacob the dish and the bread that she had prepared.

He went to his father and said, "Father." And he said, "Yes, which of my sons are you?" Jacob said to his father, "I am Esau, your first-born; I have done as you told me. Pray sit up and eat of my game, that you may give me your innermost blessing." Isaac said to his son, "How did you succeed so quickly, my son?" And he said, "Because the Lord your God granted me good fortune." Isaac said to Jacob, "Come closer that I may feel you, my son—whether you are really my son Esau or not." So Jacob drew close to his father Isaac, who felt him and wondered. "The voice is the voice of Jacob, yet the hands are the hands of Esau." He did not recognize him, because his hands were hairy like those of his brother Esau; and so he blessed him.

He asked, "Are you really my son Esau?" And when he said, "I am," he said, "Serve me and let me eat of my son's game that I may give you my innermost blessing." So he served him and he ate, and he brought him wine and he drank. Then his father Isaac said to him, "Come close and kiss me, my son"; and he went up and kissed him. And he smelled his clothes and he blessed him, saying, "Ah, the smell of my son is like the smell of the fields that the Lord has blessed.

> "May God give you
> Of the dew of heaven and the fat of the earth,
> Abundance of new grain and wine.
> Let peoples serve you,
> And nations bow to you;
> Be master over your brothers,
> And let your mother's sons bow to you.
> Cursed be they who curse you,
> Blessed they who bless you."

No sooner had Jacob left the presence of his father Isaac—after Isaac had finished blessing Jacob—than his brother Esau came back from his hunt. He too prepared a dish and brought it to his father. And he said to his father, "Let my father sit up and eat of his son's game, so that you may give me your innermost blessing." His father Isaac said to him, "Who are you?" And he said, "I am your son, Esau, your first-born!" Isaac was seized with very violent trembling. "Who was it then," he demanded, "that hunted game and brought it to me? Moreover, I ate of it before you came, and I blessed him; now he must remain blessed!" When Esau heard his father's words, he burst into wild and bitter sobbing, and said to his father, "Bless me too, Father!" But he answered, "Your brother came with guile and took away your blessing." [Esau] said, "Was he, then, named Jacob that he might supplant me these two times? First he took away my birthright and now he has taken away my blessing!" And he added, "Have you not reserved a blessing for me?" Isaac answered, saying to Esau, "But I have made him master over you: I have given him all his brothers for servants, and sustained him with grain and wine. What, then, can I still do for you, my son?" And Esau said to his father, "Have you but one blessing, Father? Bless me too, Father!" And Esau wept aloud. And his father Isaac answered, saying to him,

> "See, your abode shall enjoy the fat of the earth
> And the dew of heaven above.
> Yet by your sword you shall live,
> And you shall serve your brother;
> But when you grow restive,
> You shall break his yoke from your neck."

Now Esau harbored a grudge against Jacob because of the blessing which his father had given him, and Esau said to himself, "Let but the mourning period of my father come, and I will kill my brother Jacob." When the words of her older son Esau were reported to Rebekah, she sent for her younger son Jacob and said to him, "Your brother Esau is consoling himself by planning to kill you. Now, my son, listen to me. Flee at once to Haran, to my brother Laban. Stay with him a while, until your brother's fury subsides— until your brother's anger against you subsides—and he forgets what you have done to him. Then I will fetch you from there. Let me not lose you both in one day!" Rebekah said to Isaac, "I am disgusted with my life because of the Hittite women. If Jacob marries a Hittite woman like these, from among the native women, what good will life be to me?"

Rachel and Leah (Genesis 29:1—30:24)

Jacob resumed his journey and came to the land of the Easterners. There before his eyes was a well in the open. Three flocks of sheep were lying there beside it, for the flocks were watered from that well. The stone on the mouth of the well was large. When all the flocks were gathered there, the stone would be rolled from the mouth of the well and the sheep watered; then the stone would be put back in its place on the mouth of the well.

Jacob said to them, "My friends, where are you from?" And they said, "We are from Haran." He said to them, "Do you know Laban the son of Nahor?" And they said, "Yes, we do." He continued, "Is he well?" They answered, "Yes, he is; and there is his daughter Rachel, coming with the flock." He said, "It is still broad daylight, too early to round up the animals; water the flock and take them to pasture." But they said, "We cannot, until all the flocks are rounded up; then the stone is rolled off the mouth of the well and we water the sheep."

While he was still speaking with them, Rachel came with her father's flock; for she was a shepherdess. And when Jacob saw Rachel, the daughter of his uncle Laban, and the flock of his uncle Laban, Jacob went up and rolled the stone off the mouth of the well, and watered the flock of his uncle Laban. Then Jacob kissed Rachel, and broke into tears. Jacob told Rachel that he was her father's kinsman, that he was Rebekah's son; and she ran and told her father. On hearing the news of his sister's son Jacob, Laban ran to greet him; he embraced him and kissed him, and took him into his house. He told Laban all that had happened, and Laban said to him, "You are truly my bone and flesh."

When he had stayed with him a month's time, Laban said to Jacob, "Just because you are a kinsman, should you serve me for nothing? Tell me, what shall your wages be?" Now Laban had two daughters; the name of the older one was Leah, and the name of the younger was Rachel. Leah had weak eyes; Rachel was shapely and beautiful. Jacob loved Rachel; so he answered, "I will serve you seven years for your younger daughter Rachel." Laban said, "Better that I give her to you than that I should give her to an outsider. Stay with me." So Jacob served seven years for Rachel and they seemed to him but a few days because of his love for her.

Then Jacob said to Laban, "Give me my wife, for my time is fulfilled, that I may cohabit with her." And Laban gathered all the people of the place and made a feast. When evening came, he took his daughter Leah and brought her to him; and he cohabited with her.—Laban had given his maidservant Zilpah to his daughter Leah as her maid.—When morning came, there was Leah! So he said to Laban, "What is this you have done to me? I was in your service for Rachel! Why did you deceive me?" Laban said, "It is not the practice in our place to marry off the younger before the older. Wait until the bridal week of this one is over and we will give you that one too, provided you serve me another seven years." Jacob did so; he waited out the bridal week of the one, and then he gave him his daughter Rachel as wife.—Laban had given his maidservant Bilhah to his daughter Rachel as her maid.—And Jacob cohabited with Rachel also; indeed, he loved Rachel more than Leah. And he served him another seven years.

The Lord saw that Leah was unloved and he opened her womb; but Rachel was barren. Leah conceived and bore a son, and named him Reuben; for she declared, "It means: 'The Lord has seen my affliction'; it also means: 'Now my husband will love me.'" She conceived again and bore a son, and declared, "This is because the Lord heard that I was unloved and has given me this one also"; so she named him Simeon. Again she conceived and bore a son and declared, "This time my husband will become attached to me, for I have borne him three sons." Therefore he was named Levi. She conceived again and bore a son, and declared, "This time I will praise the Lord." Therefore she named him Judah. Then she stopped bearing.

When Rachel saw that she had borne Jacob no children, she became envious of her sister; and Rachel said to Jacob, "Give me children, or I shall die." Jacob was incensed at Rachel, and said, "Can I take the place of God, who has denied you fruit of the womb?" She said, "Here is my maid Bilhah. Consort with her, that she may bear on my knees and that through her I too may have children." So she gave him her maid Bilhah as concubine, and Jacob cohabited with her. Bilhah conceived and bore Jacob a son.

And Rachel said, "God has vindicated me; indeed, He has heeded my plea and given me a son." Therefore she named him Dan. Rachel's maid Bilhah conceived again and bore Jacob a second son. And Rachel said, "A fateful contest I waged with my sister; yes, and I have prevailed." So she named him Naphtali.

When Leah saw that she had stopped bearing, she took her maid Zilpah and gave her to Jacob as concubine. And when Leah's maid Zilpah bore Jacob a son, Leah said, "What luck!" So she named him Gad. When Leah's maid Zilpah bore Jacob a second son, Leah declared, "What fortune!" meaning, "Women will deem me fortunate." So she named him Asher.

Once, at the time of the wheat harvest, Reuben came upon some mandrakes in the field and brought them to his mother Leah. Rachel said to Leah, "Please give me some of your son's mandrakes." But she said to her, "Was it not enough for you to take away my husband, that you would also take my son's mandrakes?" Rachel replied, "I promise, he shall lie with you tonight, in return for your son's mandrakes." When Jacob came home from the field in the evening, Leah went out to meet him and said, "You are to sleep with me, for I have hired you with my son's mandrakes." And he lay with her that night. God heeded Leah, and she conceived and bore him a fifth son. And Leah said, "God has given me my reward for having given my maid to my husband." So she named him Issachar. When Leah conceived again and bore Jacob a sixth son, Leah said, "God has given me a choice gift; this time my husband will exalt me, for I have borne him six sons." So she named him Zebulun. Last, she bore him a daughter, and named her Dinah.

Now God remembered Rachel; God heeded her and opened her womb. She conceived and bore a son, and said, "God has taken away my disgrace." So she named him Joseph, which is to say, "May the Lord add another son for me."

Dinah and Shechem (Genesis 34:1–31)

Now Dinah, the daughter whom Leah had borne to Jacob, went out to visit the daughters of the land. Shechem son of Hamor the

Hivite, chief of the country, saw her, and took her and lay with her by force. Being strongly drawn to Dinah daughter of Jacob, and in love with the maiden, he spoke to the maiden tenderly. So Shechem said to his father Hamor, "Get me this girl as a wife."

Jacob heard that he had defiled his daughter Dinah; but since his sons were in the field with his cattle, Jacob kept silent until they came home. Then Shechem's father Hamor came out to Jacob to speak to him. Meanwhile Jacob's sons, having heard the news, came in from the field. The men were distressed and very angry, because he had committed an outrage in Israel by lying with Jacob's daughter—a thing not to be done.

And Hamor spoke with them, saying, "My son Shechem longs for your daughter. Please give her to him in marriage. Intermarry with us: give your daughters to us, and take our daughters for yourselves: You will dwell among us, and the land will be open before you; settle, move about, and acquire holdings in it." Then Shechem said to her father and brothers, "Do me this favor, and I will pay whatever you tell me. Ask of me a bride-price ever so high, as well as gifts, and I will pay what you tell me; only give me the maiden for a wife."

Jacob's sons answered Shechem and his father Hamor—speaking with guile because he had defiled their sister Dinah—and said to them, "We cannot do this thing, to give our sister to a man who is uncircumcised, for that is a disgrace among us. Only on this condition will we agree with you; that you will become like us in that every male among you is circumcised. Then we will give our daughters to you and take your daughters to ourselves; and we will dwell among you and become as one kindred. But if you will not listen to us and become circumcised, we will take our daughter and go."

Their words pleased Hamor and Hamor's son Shechem. And the youth lost no time in doing the thing, for he wanted Jacob's daughter. Now he was the most respected in his father's house. So Hamor and his son Shechem went to the public place of their town and spoke to their fellow townsmen, saying, "These people are our friends; let them settle in the land and move about in it, for the land is large enough for them; we will take their daughters to ourselves as wives and give our daughters to them. But only on this condition will the men agree with us to dwell among us and be as one kindred: that all our males become circumcised as they are circumcised. Their cattle and substance and all their beasts will be ours, if we only agree to their terms, so that they will settle among us." All who went out of the gate of his town heeded Hamor and his son Shechem, and all males, all those who went out of the gate of his town, were circumcised.

On the third day, when they were in pain, Simeon and Levi, two of Jacob's sons, brothers of Dinah, took each his sword, came upon the city unmolested, and slew all the males. They put Hamor and his son Shechem to the sword, took Dinah out of Shechem's house, and went away. The other sons of Jacob came upon the slain and plundered the town, because their sister had been defiled. They seized their flocks and herds and asses, all that was inside the town and outside; all their wealth, all their children, and their wives, all that was in the houses, they took as captives and booty.

Jacob said to Simeon and Levi, "You have brought trouble on me, making me odious among the inhabitants of the land, the Canaanites and the Perizzites; my men are few in number, so that if they unite against me and attack me, I and my house will be destroyed." But they answered, "Should our sister be treated like a whore?"

Joseph and His Brothers (Genesis 37:1–36)

Now Jacob was settled in the land where his father had sojourned, the land of Canaan. This, then, is the line of Jacob:

At seventeen years of age, Joseph tended the flocks with his brothers, as a helper to the sons of his father's wives Bilhah and Zilpah. And Joseph brought bad reports of them to their father. Now Israel loved Joseph best of all his sons, for he was the child of his old age; and he had made him an ornamented tunic. And when his brothers saw that their father loved him more than any of his brothers, they hated him so that they could not speak a friendly word to him.

Once Joseph had a dream which he told to his brothers; and they hated him even more. He said to them, "Hear this dream which I have dreamed: There we were binding sheaves in the field, when suddenly my sheaf stood up and remained upright; then your sheaves gathered around and bowed low to my sheaf." His brothers answered, "Do you mean to reign over us? Do you mean to rule over us?" And they hated him even more for his talk about his dreams.

He dreamed another dream and told it to his brothers, saying, "Look, I have had another dream: And this time, the sun, the moon, and eleven stars were bowing down to me." And when he told it to his father and brothers, his father berated him. "What," he said to him, "is this dream you have dreamed? Are we to come, I and your mother and your brothers, and bow low to you to the ground?" So his brothers were wrought up at him, and his father kept the matter in mind.

One time, when his brothers had gone to pasture their father's flock at Shechem, Israel said to Joseph, "Your brothers are pasturing at Shechem. Come, I will send you to them." He answered, "I am ready." And he said to him, "Go and see how your brothers are and how the flocks are faring, and bring me back word." So he sent him from the valley of Hebron.

When he reached Shechem, a man came upon him wandering in the fields. The man asked him, "What are you looking for?" He answered, "I am looking for my brothers. Could you tell me where they are pasturing?" The man said, "They have gone from here, for I heard them say: Let us go to Dothan." So Joseph followed his brothers and found them at Dothan.

They saw him from afar, and before he came close to them they conspired to kill him. They said to one another, "Here comes that dreamer! Come now, let us kill him and throw him into one of the pits; and we can say, 'A savage beast devoured him.' We shall see what comes of his dreams!" But when Reuben heard it, he tried to save him from them. He said, "Let us not take his life." And

Reuben went on, "Shed no blood! Cast him into that pit out in the wilderness, but do not touch him yourselves"—intending to save him from them and restore him to his father. When Joseph came up to his brothers, they stripped Joseph of his tunic, the ornamented tunic that he was wearing, and took him and cast him into the pit. The pit was empty; there was no water in it.

Then they sat down to a meal. Looking up, they saw a caravan of Ishmaelites coming from Gilead, their camels bearing gum, balm, and ladanum to be taken to Egypt. Then Judah said to his brothers, "What do we gain by killing our brother and covering up his blood? Come, let us sell him to the Ishmaelites, but let us not do away with him ourselves. After all, he is our brother, our own flesh." His brothers agreed. When Midianite traders passed by, they pulled Joseph up out of the pit. They sold Joseph for twenty pieces of silver to the Ishmaelites, who brought Joseph to Egypt.

When Reuben returned to the pit and saw that Joseph was not in the pit, he rent his clothes. Returning to his brothers, he said, "The boy is gone! Now, what am I to do?" Then they took Joseph's tunic, slaughtered a kid, and dipped the tunic in the blood. They had the ornamented tunic taken to their father, and they said, "We found this. Please examine it; is it your son's tunic or not?" He recognized it, and said, "My son's tunic! A savage beast devoured him! Joseph was torn by a beast!" Jacob rent his clothes, put sackcloth on his loins, and observed mourning for his son many days. All his sons and daughters sought to comfort him; but he refused to be comforted, saying, "No, I will go down mourning to my son in Sheol." Thus his father bewailed him.

The Midianites, meanwhile, sold him in Egypt to Potiphar, a courtier of Pharaoh and his chief steward

Tamar and Judah (Genesis 38:1–30)

About that time Judah left his brothers and camped near a certain Adullamite whose name was Hirah. There Judah saw the daughter of a certain Canaanite whose name was Shua, and he married her and cohabited with her. She conceived and bore a son, and he named him Er. She conceived again and bore a son, and named him Onan. Once again she bore a son, and named him Shelah; he was at Chezib when she bore him.

Judah got a wife for Er his first-born; her name was Tamar. But Er, Judah's first-born, was displeasing to the Lord, and the Lord took his life. Then Judah said to Onan, "Join with your brother's wife and do your duty by her as a brother-in-law, and provide offspring for your brother." But Onan, knowing that the seed would not count as his, let it go to waste whenever he joined with his brother's wife, so as not to provide offspring for his brother. What he did was displeasing to the Lord, and He took his life also. Then Judah said to his daughter-in-law Tamar, "Stay as a widow in your father's house until my son Shelah grows up"—for he thought, "He too might die like his brothers." So Tamar went to live in her father's house.

A long time afterward, Shua's daughter, the wife of Judah, died. When his period of mourning was over, Judah went up to Timnah to his sheepshearers, together with his friend Hirah the Adullamite. And Tamar was told, "Your father-in-law is coming up to Timnah for the sheepshearing." So she took off her widow's garb, covered her face with a veil, and, wrapping herself up, sat down at the entrance to Enaim, which is on the road to Timnah; for she saw that Shelah was grown up, yet she had not been given to him as wife. When Judah saw her, he took her for a harlot; for she had covered her face. So he turned aside to her by the road and said, "Here, let me sleep with you"—for he did not know that she was his daughter-in-law. "What," she asked, "will you pay for sleeping with me?" He replied, "I will send a kid from my flock." But she said, "You must leave a pledge until you have sent it." And he said, "What pledge shall I give you?" She replied, "Your seal and cord, and the staff which you carry." So he gave them to her and slept with her, and she conceived by him. Then she went on her way. She took off her veil and again put on her widow's garb.

Judah sent the kid by his friend the Adullamite, to redeem the pledge from the woman; but he could not find her. He inquired of the people of that town, "Where is the cult prostitute, the one at Enaim, by the road?" But they said, "There has been no prostitute here." So he returned to Judah and said, "I could not find her; moreover, the townspeople said: There has been no prostitute here." Judah said, "Let her keep them, lest we become a laughingstock. I did send her this kid, but you did not find her."

About three months later, Judah was told, "Your daughter-in-law Tamar has played the harlot; in fact, she is with child by harlotry." "Bring her out," said Judah, "and let her be burned." As she was being brought out, she sent this message to her father-in-law, "I am with child by the man to whom these belong." And she added, "Examine these: whose seal and cord and staff are these?" Judah recognized them, and said, "She is more in the right than I, inasmuch as I did not give her to my son Shelah." And he was not intimate with her again.

When the time came for her to give birth, there were twins in her womb! While she was in labor, one of them put out his hand, and the midwife tied a crimson thread on that hand, to signify: This one came out first. But just then he drew back his hand, and out came his brother; and she said, "What a breach you have made for yourself!" So he was named Perez. Afterward his brother came out, on whose hand was the crimson thread; he was named Zerah.

Joseph and the Wife of Potiphar (Genesis 39:1–23)

When Joseph was taken down to Egypt, a certain Egyptian, Potiphar, a courtier of Pharaoh and his chief steward, bought him from the Ishmaelites who had brought him there. The Lord was with Joseph, and he was a successful man; and he stayed in the house of his Egyptian master. And when his master saw that the Lord was with him and that the Lord lent success to everything he undertook, he took a liking to Joseph. He made him his personal attendant and put him in charge of his household, placing in his hands all that he owned. And from the time that the Egyptian put him in charge of his household and of all that he owned, the Lord blessed his house for Joseph's sake, so that the blessing of the Lord was upon everything that he owned, in the house and outside. He left all that he had in Joseph's hands and, with him there, he paid attention to nothing save the food that he ate. Now Joseph was well built and handsome.

After a time, his master's wife cast her eyes upon Joseph and said, "Lie with me." But he refused. He said to his master's wife, "Look, with me here, my master gives no thought to anything in this house, and all that he owns he has placed in my hands. He wields no more authority in this house than I, and he has withheld nothing from me except yourself, since you are his wife. How then could I do this most wicked thing, and sin before God?" And much as she coaxed Joseph day after day, he did not yield to her request to lie beside her, to be with her.

One such day, he came into the house to do his work. None of the household being there inside, she caught hold of him by his garment and said, "Lie with me!" But he left his garment in her hand and got away and fled outside. When she saw that he had left it in her hand and had fled outside, she called out to her servants and said to them, "Look, he had to bring us a Hebrew to dally with us! This one came to lie with me; but I screamed loud. And when he heard me screaming at the top of my voice, he left his garment with me and got away and fled outside." She kept his garment beside her, until his master came home. Then she told him the same story, saying, "The Hebrew slave whom you brought into our house came to me to dally with me; but when I screamed at the top of my voice, he left his garment with me and fled outside."

When his master heard the story that his wife told him, namely, "Thus and so your slave did to me," he was furious. So Joseph's master had him put in prison, where the king's prisoners were confined. But even while he was there in prison, the Lord was with Joseph: He extended kindness to him and disposed the chief jailer favorably toward him. The chief jailer put in Joseph's charge all the prisoners who were in that prison, and he was the one to carry out everything that was done there. The chief jailer did not supervise anything that was in Joseph's charge, because the Lord was with him, and whatever he did the Lord made successful.

CHAPTER 2

Establishing a Framework

WE'D LIKE YOU TO ask yourself a simple question. What do you know about the book of Genesis?

Even if you never studied it as a child, you are most likely familiar with the iconic images and metaphors Genesis has given to our culture. The story of Adam and Eve and the concept of original sin. The garden of Eden as the idyllic paradise par excellence. The snake as the ultimate symbol of evil. Even the story of the great flood and of the animals coming two by two to enter the ark. Be it Shakespeare's *Hamlet*, Steinbeck's *The Grapes of Wrath*, or even Veronica Roth's *Divergent*, classic and contemporary literature alike are replete with biblical imagery culled from Genesis.

If you did study Genesis as a child, perhaps your recollections go deeper. You may remember the days of creation and the colorful illustrations you drew for your parents to hang on the refrigerator door. Maybe you remember the story of Abraham and Isaac heading toward the mountain where Abraham had every intention, so it seemed, to sacrifice his beloved son. And maybe, just maybe, you remember Joseph and his amazing "Technicolor Dreamcoat"—although it was certainly not called that when you were a child.

What you surely do not remember are stories of incest, of concubines and threesomes, and of dysfunctional and troubled marriages. There could have been stories of sibling rivalry. After all, what child does not have an annoying older or younger sibling? But stories of one sibling murdering another, of siblings threatening and plotting to kill one another, of selling a brother into slavery? Not likely. And if you were taught any of this, it was surely in a most childlike and simplistic fashion.

Here, then, is the problem religious leaders and teachers of the biblical narrative face when interacting with adults: Adults think they know the general narrative of Genesis, but they do not. Worse still, they must unlearn the Bible of their youth in order to see how relevant it truly is for them today. As we have already noted, this is no easy task.

Fully aware of the challenges, we would like to propose a framework for relearning Genesis. In doing so, we hope to make clear not only *how* but *why* one should endeavor to do so.

So how does one go about learning the biblical text? The Jewish rabbinic tradition suggests that there are actually five ways of doing so: interpreting the verses literally, viewing the Bible as a legal code, understanding the Bible as a morality tale, reading it as a tale, and seeing it as a text laced with overarching themes. While there is a time and a place for interpreting the Bible both literally and as a legal code (especially the last four books of the Pentateuch, Exodus through Deuteronomy), we wish to focus on the last three approaches.[1] In particular, we are interested in examining the biblical text as a morality tale. Indeed, it is our contention that the book of Genesis can and should be learned as a morality tale because its stories are still applicable for the modern times in which we live.

As the Bible itself attests, "there is nothing new under the sun" (Ecclesiastes 1:9). So many of the issues that political, community, and even religious leaders see as unique to our times are discussed at length in the book of Genesis. Children miss this. Adults, when they relearn Genesis as the sophisticated narrative that it is, quickly see in it a series of stories that highlight the just

---

1. Learning the Pentateuch as a legal code is foundational for the Jewish faith because the Pentateuch ultimately forms the basic law book for Judaism.

and the right thing to do. They also see that law is *not* the focus of Genesis. The book does not command us what to do.[2] It instead sets forth a template for individuals to use when making decisions and illustrates for them the need to be mindful of the real-life (but *not* legal) consequences of those decisions.

Consider but one example. In chapter 12 of Genesis, Abraham decides to go down to Egypt and then opts to tell people that Sarah is his sister, not his wife:

> There was a famine in the land, and Abram went down to Egypt to sojourn there, for the famine was severe in the land. As he was about to enter Egypt, he said to his wife Sarai, "I know what a beautiful woman you are. If the Egyptians see you, and think, 'She is his wife,' they will kill me and let you live. Please say that you are my sister, that it may go well with me because of you, and that I may remain alive thanks to you" (Genesis 12:10–13)

Jewish tradition sees the famine in the land of Canaan as one of the ten times Abraham was famously tested by God: "Our forefather Abraham was tested with ten trials and withstood all of them. This demonstrates how beloved our forefather Abraham of blessed memory was [to God]" (Ethics of the Fathers 5:4). But the classical medieval commentators on the text disagree as to the outcome of this particular test. Most note that Abraham passes the test. How so? He does not question God and goes on to Egypt in order to survive. Doing so is simply a logical response to the famine. The countervailing view is that Abraham fails the test. It is true that he faces a real dilemma. Staying in Canaan means starving to death. Going down to Egypt may result in his death, but Abraham does not handle either option particularly well. To those who see Abraham as failing this test, his first failure—or perhaps his sin—is a lack of trust that God will save him from the famine. Yet the greater sin in the eyes of these commentators, his moral shortcoming as they see it, is that Abraham puts Sarah in danger. Abraham takes

---

2. According to the Jewish tradition, Genesis contains only three commandments: procreation (Genesis 1:28), circumcision for males (Genesis 17:14), and the prohibition against eating the sciatic nerve (Genesis 32:33).

Sarah, the most righteous, the most beautiful woman of this time, to Egypt. To Egypt? A land known for its sexual perversions?[3] How could this happen? It can only be that this entire incident is a test; if not, why would God want Sarah to go to Egypt?

Seeing Genesis as a morality tale also encourages us to learn its narratives as literature. Literary themes run through vast sections of the Bible, and one can learn the Bible, so to speak, as literature. One of the literary themes that runs through the book of Genesis is the triumph of the younger son over the older son. Cain is the only son in the book who is not vanquished by his younger brother, but this is only because he *kills* his brother. This theme crops up in several different stories, and in every story other than that of Cain and Abel, the younger son triumphs over the older. The astute Bible student with an adult perspective should ask: "Why is this theme running throughout the book of Genesis? What does God want us to learn from this pattern? Couldn't God have given us one story that deals with a particular problem and thus spell out His preferred approach for handling the issue?" He could have. But the fact that the literary themes—including the triumph of the younger brother over the firstborn, which we will discuss in greater detail later—are addressed in a variety of stories forces us to focus on a given problem from several different perspectives: literary, legally, and morally.

Once we see how these broad literary themes appear in several different stories, we come to the realization that the piecemeal way in which we often study the Bible—story by story, chapter by chapter, book by book—can cause us to miss the big picture. To illustrate the point, let's return to our example. Even if one notes the very obvious theme of the younger son prevailing over the older,

3. The notion that ancient Egypt was a highly promiscuous culture is frequently articulated by the medieval biblical commentators. Scholarly research also supports the view that "widespread and gross immorality" flourished in ancient Egypt. "Prostitution was probably common and among the ranks of the courtesans were many married women whose husbands had left them, and who wandered about the country practising [sic] their profession. An overlord might and probably did at times abuse his power by making the daughters of his inferiors subjects of his passion." See Reynolds, "Sex Morals," 21.

the full force of this thematic pattern would be missed if the reader takes note of it only in the context of a single story. To fully appreciate this theme, one must also compare these stories of sibling rivalry with the law.

Consider that the Bible, when it delineates the rules of inheritance, mandates that the firstborn inherits double: "Instead he must accept the first-born, the son of the unloved one, and allot to him a double portion of all he possesses, since he is the first fruit of his vigor, the birthright is his due" (Deuteronomy 21:17). How do we harmonize this law with the sibling rivalry stories in Genesis? If the firstborn son is entitled to a double inheritance, why does he never really triumph in these tales? Is this double portion of material goods a way to quantify winning? Or are we dealing with something else here? As we contemplate such questions, we must never forget that the same Source Who gave us the stories gave us the law.

From our many years of teaching, we have seen how people tend to learn the Bible in very compartmentalized analyses of its narratives, especially in public or group settings. As a result, people sometimes fail to step back and look at the bigger picture. Our goal in presenting this overview in general and this book in its entirety is to help our readers learn how and when to look at the big picture as they relate to the book of Genesis.

We make no claims that we can and will do so completely, nor is this book meant to be an encyclopedia of issues that run throughout the book of Genesis. Rather, we will cover major literary themes we see appearing over and over in Genesis. These touch on human sexuality, marriage and reproductive issues, and sibling rivalry. What is the common thread that ties these literary themes together? In each, Genesis shows us how individuals, and the society in which they live, are to function when actions are governed not by law but by mutual consent.

There is one last point worth noting as we establish a framework for our discussion of the Genesis stories. The families we meet in Genesis are defined by complicated interactions between spouses (and sometimes with other consenting adults who join the marriage), between parents and children, and between siblings. This means that the tale of a single biblical family, that of Jacob, for example, has much to teach us about sexuality, about marriage, and about sibling rivalry. We will examine such stories from different perspectives throughout this book. This, we believe, is the proper approach to grasp the themes that run through these stories.

In the end, we believe the topics we will analyze are grounded in central themes that are interesting and that shape the narrative thrust of the book of Genesis. We should also point out that most of the topics herein will be discussed through the filter of modernity; that is, we hope to show that the problems many see as plaguing us today are not new and that they are instead part of the very fabric of the biblical text. We further hope that it becomes clear to our readers that one can have a goodly life, blessed with a relationship with the Divine, even if he or she comes from a complex family.

Chapter 3

Human Sexuality

WHILE SHE MIGHT ARGUE to the contrary, Pamela Druckerman is the embodiment of the times in which we live.

She is an accomplished woman, who earned a Bachelor of Arts in philosophy from Colgate University and a Master of International Affairs from Columbia University. She has won an Emmy and is a best-selling author.[1] Her op-eds, articles, and reviews have appeared in the *Atlantic*, *Harper's*, *Marie Claire*, *Vanity Fair* France, *Madame Figaro*, the *Washington Post*, the *Guardian*, the *Financial Times*, the *Times* (UK), the *Sunday Times* (UK), *New York* magazine, and many other publications. She has appeared as a commentator on *All Things Considered*, *Morning Edition*, BBC *Woman's Hour*, *Good Morning America*, the *Today* show, CNN, CNBC, MSNBC, PRI, the CBC, Europe1, *Le Grand Journal*, *On n'est pas couché*, and Oprah.com. She is currently a Contributing Opinion Writer for the *New York Times*, where she writes about France, cross-cultural issues, and daily life.

---

1. Her Emmy win in 2016 was for *The Forger*, a sixteen-minute documentary. *Druckerman, Bringing Up Bébé* was a number one best seller in the UK (*Sunday Times*), a top-ten best seller in the United States (*New York Times*), and has appeared on best-seller lists in Germany, Russia, and Brazil.

She planned a sexual threesome with with her husband and another woman for her husband's fortieth birthday and wrote about it for *Esquire* magazine in 2015.[2]

Here is how she describes her marriage prior to this escapade: "I should say that we are normally quite dull. We don't swing or have an open marriage. We're rarely even awake past 10 p.m. Although I wrote a book about infidelity around the world, I ended up concluding that fidelity is quite a good idea. So far, it has been for us. This wouldn't technically be cheating, but it's not textbook monogamy either." No, it's not. Nor is it illegal, a point which we will return to shortly. But there may well be consequences, something Druckerman does not ignore. When scouting out potential female partners for this joint venture, she encounters a friend of a friend she has met at dinner parties but whose name she can never remember. (Her name is Emma.) After clearing this potential partner with her husband, Druckerman meets her for lunch.

> I think she gets that I'm propositioning her, but instead of taking the bait, she becomes the Cassandra of threesomes. She describes the rogue ex-boyfriend who pressured her to go to bed with him and his other lover, and the friends of hers who swapped partners and never swapped back. She says that I'll be scarred by images of my husband doing unspeakable things to another woman. "And what if it's someone who's incredibly hot? How could you possibly handle that?" she asks, a bit insultingly.

Druckerman sees the likelihood of disaster that a hook-up with Emma portends, but she is undeterred. Instead, she is energized and even empowered by her mission.

> My new man's-eye view of the world is thrilling. I notice women everywhere—at the photo shop, in line at the supermarket. I even scan my book group—middle-aged expatriates who like to read about the Holocaust—for candidates. I have a belated feminist revelation: Women don't demand raises and promotions because we're

2. Druckerman, "Why I Let My Husband Have a Threesome."

trained to sit pretty and let someone else chase us. In my
new role as decider, I don't care what anyone thinks of
me. I just go after what I want from them. It's refreshing
to have some time off from wondering whether I look fat.

Going after what she wants ultimately means searching for possible partners online, and there Druckerman discovers "N." A series of email exchanges becomes a series of lunch dates, which leads to the birthday celebration of her husband's dreams. We will leave it to interested readers to peruse Druckerman's article for the details of what followed. For our purposes, we are more interested in the aftermath of the experience.

> N. seems very pleased too. On the walk home, she says
> she's surprised by how erotic she found the whole experi-
> ence, especially being with me. I'm flattered to have con-
> verted her. But I feel like the Christian missionary who
> realizes—just after the big revival—that she's actually
> more of a Jew. I'm not nearly as gay as I thought I was. I'd
> always felt that there might be something else out there.
> Now—and not just by the process of elimination—I'm
> struck by how emphatically I want my husband. I'm left
> feeling unsettled. I can't wait to shower. Sadly, I'm more
> conventional than I'd thought. In theory, I didn't mind
> sharing my husband for an afternoon. In practice, I was
> shaken up. I wasn't bored; I was bothered.

There are some even today who may be shocked that this sort of thing goes on, especially in such a laissez-faire manner. (Druckerman was, after all, living in Paris!) Others might be bothered by how open and, they might say, how brazen Druckerman was. (Publishing such details in *Esquire*!) And still others may be disturbed that our society simply does not care about such things.

Druckerman's story is, for these reasons, one for our times. Let us be clear. Whether you admire her or are outraged by her, Druckerman and her husband did nothing illegal. She merely helped her husband live out his fantasy, and they seem to have emerged unscathed. We would argue that, by engaging in this threesome, the Druckermans represent the sexual mores of many in our modern times: liberated, curious, unwilling to deny themselves any pleasure, seeing sexuality as fluid. Druckerman did acknowledge the possible consequences of her actions, but that acknowledgement did not deter her, just as it did not deter many of the characters in the Genesis stories we will discuss below.

Before delving into these stories, we would like to quickly look at some of the current research on sexuality and sexual conduct in America today in order to better understand the extent to which life in America mirrors the cultures depicted in Genesis.

A logical starting point for considering trends in sexual behavior is premarital sex.[3] In a 2015 paper published in the *Archives of Sexual Behavior*, researchers from San Diego State University, Florida Atlantic University, and CUNY reviewed the literature on sexual behavior generally and analyzed data from the nationally representative General Social Survey (GSS), a research project that resulted in perhaps the most complete record of public opinion shifts in the United States on many issues.[4] While the researchers note that "the current research literature provides contradictory evidence on whether sexual attitudes and behaviors have grown more or less permissive in recent years," their findings are conclusive regarding premarital sex: it is now normative behavior.[5] Given that men and women typically marry in their mid-to-late twenties, this should come as no shock. It is also a reflection of the Genesis-like status of American culture. In Genesis, as in America today, sexual choices are governed not by a code of law but by the individual's sense of what is right for him or her.

3. Neither of us are researchers or social scientists. Some readers may take issue with the studies we have opted to use to make our points. Their criticism may or may not be valid, but we found the studies we relied on to be readily available and straightforward in their language and findings.

4. Twenge et al., "Changes." The GSS has asked the same four questions relating to sexual attitudes since 1972; it added more questions about sexual practices in 1988.

5. Twenge et al., "Changes," 2276, 2278 (direct quote on 2276). Parenthetically, as will be clear from the Genesis stories we examine, especially those involving the pre-flood era, premarital sex was common.

These findings led the researchers to another question, namely, how often do people have sex and with whom?[6]

As one might suspect, the number of sexual partners has increased. Specifically, the total number of sexual partners individuals report having from age eighteen increased from 7.17 in the late 1980s (11.42 for men versus 3.54 for women) to 11.22 in the 2010s (18.22 for men versus 5.55 for women). The rates of casual sex have also increased. Among individuals aged eighteen to twenty-nine reporting "non-partner sex," 35 percent of GenXers in the late 1980s had sex with a casual date or pickup (44 percent of men versus 19 percent of women), compared to 45 percent of Millennials in the 2010s (55 percent of men versus 31 percent of women).[7]

At this point, you are probably asking yourself, what does all of this have to do with studying the Bible? Everything, actually, because all this and much more is there in Genesis when one is able and willing to read it as an adult.

Adultery, threesomes, incest, rape, hedonist behavior; it is all there in Genesis. And it is not there because Genesis is a legal code that comes to prohibit such behavior. It does no such thing. Instead, it presents a series of narratives involving human sexuality to teach us about the very real harm that can come to the relationships we treasure most when we focus on what is legal and illegal instead of what is appropriate and correct.

Let us therefore begin to unpack the twenty-first-century morality tale that Genesis truly is. A careful adult reader of Genesis will quickly notice that tales of sexuality run throughout the book. To facilitate our analysis and to better grasp the lessons to be learned from these stories, we have grouped them into three broad categories.

6. As we will soon discuss, polyamorous relationships permeate Genesis, so this question is not applicable to the biblical narratives we examine.

7. Twenge et al., "Changes," 6.

Non-Monogamous Relationships

The first is threesomes—but not of the sort Druckerman planned. These threesomes are not the fulfillment of someone's long-held sexual fantasy but are entered into with careful calculations and for seemingly sound reasons. Nonetheless, each has a detrimental impact on the relationship between husband and wife. Case in point: Abraham and Sarah.

On three separate occasions, this patriarchal couple invite a third person into the most personal aspect of their lives. We briefly alluded to the first in the previous chapter, when Abraham and Sarah are forced to go down to Egypt in the face of a serious famine in Canaan.

> There was a famine in the land, and Abram went down to Egypt to sojourn there, for the famine was severe in the land. As he was about to enter Egypt, he said to his wife Sarai, "I know what a beautiful woman you are. If the Egyptians see you, and think, 'She is his wife,' they will kill me and let you live. Please say that you are my sister, that it may go well with me because of you, and that I may remain alive thanks to you." (Genesis 12:10–13)

As portrayed in these verses, this seems cold and calculated. They face starvation if they remain in Canaan, yet Egypt, where they can find food to eat, holds a real and likely fatal outcome for Abraham. That is quite an unpleasant set of options, so this quick-thinking couple comes up with a third: find a powerful patron who can guarantee their safety and their lives. What can they offer as compensation? Sarah.

Sarah must have consented to this deal, notwithstanding the silence of the verses in this matter. Genesis, as we have already stated and will soon demonstrate, is all about consent, especially in sexual matters. As will become very apparent when we examine the story of how Potiphar's wife sought to seduce Joseph, non-consensual sex, even in Egypt, was a red line not to be crossed.[8]

8. The laws of Ancient Egypt relating to public morality may be briefly summarized as follows: "According to the 'unwritten law' of the best public

At first glance, their plan seems to work. "Pharaoh's courtiers saw her and praised her to Pharaoh, and the woman was taken into Pharaoh's palace. And because of her, it went well with Abram; he acquired sheep, oxen, asses, male and female slaves, she-asses, and camels" (Genesis 12:15–16). A simple reading of the story suggests that Abraham and Sarah did not conduct themselves as husband and wife in Egypt, just as it hints at sexual intimacy between the Egyptian monarch and Sarah. Yet God seems rather displeased by this arrangement: "But the Lord afflicted Pharaoh and his household with mighty plagues on account of Sarai, the wife of Abram" (Genesis 12:17).[9]

Understandably, Pharaoh is a bit perturbed by how this all turns out. "Pharaoh sent for Abram and said, 'What is this you have done to me! Why did you not tell me that she was your wife? Why did you say, 'She is my sister,' so that I took her as my wife? Now, here is your wife; take her and begone!'" (Genesis 12:18–19). And so, under royal escort, Abraham and Sarah return to Canaan, their marriage seemingly intact and their financial assets greatly increased (Genesis 12:20). Yet looks can be deceiving. Perhaps, as in the case of Druckerman and her husband, the marriage of Abraham and Sarah survived this dalliance, but a template was set. Here Sarah is urged to give her consent to bringing a third party into her marriage bed. In the next tale, that involving Hagar, it is Sarah who takes the initiative and insists on again bringing another into their home and their bed.

> Sarai, Abram's wife, had borne him no children. She had an Egyptian maidservant whose name was Hagar. And Sarai said to Abram, "Look, the Lord has kept me from bearing. Consort with my maid; perhaps I shall have a son through her." And Abram heeded Sarai's request.

sentiment, as stated in the Maxims of Ani on a Boulaq papyrus, immorality was strongly condemned." See Reynolds, "Sex Morals," 20.

9. The traditional Jewish commentaries reject the notion that Sarah and Pharaoh had a sexual relationship, pointing to the "mighty plagues" mentioned in this verse as proof. They maintain Pharaoh was struck by these unnamed afflictions before he could have sex with Sarah, not afterward, as a form of punishment.

> So Sarai, Abram's wife, took her maid, Hagar the Egyptian—after Abram had dwelt in the land of Canaan ten years—and gave her to her husband Abram as concubine. He cohabited with Hagar and she conceived; and when she saw that she had conceived, her mistress was lowered in her esteem. And Sarai said to Abram, "The wrong done me is your fault! I myself put my maid in your bosom; now that she sees that she is pregnant, I am lowered in her esteem. The Lord decide between you and me!" Abram said to Sarai, "Your maid is in your hands. Deal with her as you think right." Then Sarai treated her harshly, and she ran away from her (Genesis 16:1–6).

The Abraham-Sarah-Hagar triangle is very much about personal choices, not about law. As such, it fits nicely into the overall Genesis narrative. Genesis nonetheless does seem to set forth a preference for interpersonal relations between men and women when it states that "a man leaves his father and mother and clings to his wife, so that they become one flesh" (Genesis 2:24). Why, then, do Abraham and Sarah veer away from the preferred paradigm a second time?

Once again, this is not a tale of lust or desire gone astray. Abraham and Sarah seem to be making a very practical choice, or at least Sarah is. They are childless but, as the ones tasked with spreading awareness of the one true God to humankind, they feel a deep need to have an heir, one who will understand their mission and who can be properly trained to carry on with it.

True, this triangle begins simply enough: "Consort with my maid; perhaps I shall have a son through her." Yet, as will become very, very clear throughout the overall Genesis storyline, having multiple wives is an absolute disaster on many levels: socially, culturally, spiritually, emotionally, and psychologically. Just consider the aftermath of Abraham taking on Hagar as a concubine.

- Hagar quickly conceives and, as a result, "her mistress was lowered in her esteem" (Genesis 16:4).

- Sarah, embarrassed by her own inability to conceive and certainly jealous of Hagar's relationship with her husband, complains bitterly to Abraham (Genesis 16:5). She then treats Hagar so harshly that Hagar runs away (Genesis 16:6).

- Ultimately, Sarah does have a son on her own, but she views the relationship between the two boys—her biological child, Isaac, and her surrogate child, Hagar's son—as so harmful that she demands Abraham send away this rival (Genesis 21:9–10).

- This demand so distressed Abraham that he was unable to act.[10] Only when God Himself tells him to "do whatever Sarah tells you" does Abraham find the strength to banish Hagar and Ishmael (Genesis 21:11–12).

Unlike the sexual compromises Abraham and Sarah made in Egypt, this threesome has an immediate and obvious detrimental impact on their marriage. One would have thought that this was it; that their dalliances with polyamorous adventures was over, but no, there was still one more awaiting them. "Abraham journeyed from there to the region of the Negeb and settled between Kadesh and Shur. While he was sojourning in Gerar, Abraham said of Sarah his wife, 'She is my sister.' So King Abimelech of Gerar had Sarah brought to him" (Genesis 20:1–2). It is unclear why Abraham and Sarah travel to Gerar. There is no famine, as there was when they went down to Egypt. It could be, as some speculate, that they were eager to distance themselves from the region in the aftermath of God's destruction of Sodom and Gomorrah (Genesis 19:24–25). Whatever the reason for their move, one can only wonder, why repeat the "she is my sister" ruse?

In a kind of postscript, after their ruse is exposed, Abraham claims that he feared for his life: "'I thought,' said Abraham, 'surely there is no fear of God in this place, and they will kill me because of my wife.'" (Genesis 20:11). He continues that this has been their modus operandi for years: "So when God made me wander from my father's house, I said to her, 'Let this be the kindness that you

---

10. Some maintain that this was one of the ten tests Abraham famously faced.

shall do me: whatever place we come to, say there of me: He is my brother.'" (Genesis 20:13).

Yes, it is possible that King Abimelech posed some sort of threat to Abraham, as the continuing storyline has he and his descendants doing years later to Isaac, but there is no indication of that at this point in the narrative. Could there be more to it? Could it be that the jealousy and alienation Sarah feels in the aftermath of their interactions with Hagar have left her wanting to feel desired again? Could it be that she consents to yet another threesome out of a deep sense of loneliness?

Our speculations notwithstanding, God is not so understanding or cooperative. He may not be inclined to impose a strict legal structure to govern sexual matters in Genesis, but He does insist that people act morally. And, for Him, this proposed threesome is just too much. Unlike Egypt, where the narrative itself is unclear on the question of whether Pharaoh and Sarah were sexually intimate, here God steps in before Abimelech can act upon his (and conceivably Sarah's) desires.

> But God came to Abimelech in a dream by night and said to him, "You are to die because of the woman that you have taken, for she is a married woman." Now Abimelech had not approached her. He said, "O Lord, will You slay people even though innocent? He himself said to me, 'She is my sister!' And she also said, 'He is my brother.' When I did this, my heart was blameless and my hands were clean." And God said to him in the dream, "I knew that you did this with a blameless heart, and so I kept you from sinning against Me. That was why I did not let you touch her. Therefore, restore the man's wife—since he is a prophet, he will intercede for you—to save your life. If you fail to restore her, know that you shall die, you and all that are yours" (Genesis 20:3–7).

As was the case with Pharaoh before him, Abimelech is furious with Abraham: "Then Abimelech summoned Abraham and said to him, 'What have you done to us? What wrong have I done that you should bring so great a guilt upon me and my kingdom? You have done to me things that ought not to be done'" (Genesis 20:9).

And as was the case in Egypt, Abraham and Sarah emerge from the situation financially enriched.

> Abimelech took sheep and oxen, and male and female slaves, and gave them to Abraham; and he restored his wife Sarah to him. And Abimelech said, "Here, my land is before you; settle wherever you please." And to Sarah he said, "I herewith give your brother a thousand pieces of silver; this will serve you as vindication before all who are with you, and you are cleared before everyone" (Genesis 20:14–16).

There is, however, one major difference between these two stories. After Egypt, it seems that their marriage is still healthy, that it is still working. After Gerar, it seems less so. God fulfills His promise to Sarah, and she finally has a son of her own. As a result, Hagar and Ishmael are no longer mere annoyances but threats to her biological son's future. She becomes more assertive, more demanding. She forces Abraham to banish his concubine and his firstborn son, whom he dearly loves. We believe that this merely deepens the growing rift between Abraham and Sarah. And, make no mistake, a careful reading of their story shows how deep this rift grows.

Traditional Jewish sources tell us that, when this couple first set out from Ur, headed for an unknown land, they were supportive partners with each seeing the other as a peer (Genesis 12:1). These same sources relate that the two were equally committed to teaching humanity about the one true God, with Abraham instructing the men and Sarah the women. And in the aftermath of not one, not two, but *three* polyamorous relationships, their marriage seems frayed.

On what do we base this claim? A bit of narrative and a bit of geography.

The narrative is short but striking. When Abraham faces his greatest test, the command to offer Isaac as a sacrifice, he neither consults nor informs Sarah. He simply gets up early in the morning and heads off for his task (Genesis 22:3). As for the geography, Abraham is living in Beersheba when he is told by God to bring Isaac as a sacrifice. Yet, we are also told that Sarah is living in

Hebron at the time of her death shortly after the attempted sacrifice of Isaac (Gen 23:2). Happily married couples typically do not maintain separate households.

Throughout the saga of Abraham and Sarah, we see two people making decisions that make sense to them at the time and that are entered into with full consent. All the same, the Genesis narrative has its point to make. Even things that go against no law and are based on the consent of all involved may not be the right thing to do, especially when such actions threaten the very foundations upon which one's marriage is built.

Jealousy-Riddled Relationships

The second category we have opted to use in framing our discussion of sexuality involves jealousy. Jealousy is a complex emotion, one that encompasses a range of feelings, from fear of abandonment to rage and humiliation, all of which are manifest in the many sexuality tales found in Genesis.

Let us begin with the best known and arguably least understood story in all of Genesis, that of Adam and Eve. It is a story always taught in a sanitized and childlike manner, an approach that is reflected in virtually every English translation of the tale from the original Hebrew. But it is the Hebrew, with all its nuances, that reveals the true nature of this tale.

We are all familiar with the gist of the story. God tells Adam and Eve not to eat from a particular tree, but the serpent tricks Eve into doing so. As punishment, Adam and Eve are banished from Eden, and the serpent is cursed by God: "More cursed shall you be than all cattle and all the wild beasts: On your belly shall you crawl and dirt shall you eat all the days of your life" (Genesis 1:14).

Is there really much more to the story than this? Yes, actually—quite a bit more, especially when one stops to contemplate some key but problematic Hebrew words in the story itself.

> Now the serpent was *arum* [עָרוּם] of all the wild beasts that the Lord God had made. He said to the woman, "Did God really say: 'You shall not eat of any tree of the

garden?'" The woman replied to the serpent, "We may
eat of the fruit of the other trees of the garden. It is only
about fruit of the tree in the middle of the garden that
God said: 'You shall not eat of it or touch it, lest you die.'"
And the serpent said to the woman, "You are not going to
die, but God knows that as soon as you eat of it your eyes
will be opened and you will be like divine beings who
know good and bad." When the woman saw that the tree
was good for eating and a delight to the eyes, and that
the tree was desirable as a source of wisdom, she took
of its fruit and ate. She also gave some to her husband,
and he ate. Then the eyes of both of them were opened,
and they perceived that they were naked; and they sewed
together fig leaves and made themselves loincloths (Genesis 3:1–7).

Why did we leave this Hebrew word עָרוֹם untranslated? It is a
reflection of the complexities in translating Hebrew words built
upon the three root letters ע, ר, and ם.

Biblical lexicographers have long noted that there are two distinct words in the Bible that use these three root letters. The first,
עָרוֹם (pronounced *aw-rome'*), is an adjective that is typically translated as "naked."[11] The second, עָרוּם (pronounced *aw-room'*), is also
an adjective, but it is translated as "crafty," "shrewd," or "sensible."[12]
Although the difference in vocalization between the two words is
subtle, lexicographers and translators alike see them as completely
different. Given this, it is both interesting and perplexing that the
Hebrew verses in the Adam and Eve story that use these words
seem to conflate them. Genesis 2:25 says: וַיִּהְיוּ שְׁנֵיהֶם עֲרוּמִּים הָאָדָם
וְאִשְׁתּוֹ וְלֹא יִתְבֹּשָׁשׁוּ: "The two of them were naked (*aw-roo'-mim*),
the man and his wife, yet they felt no shame," while Genesis 3:1
says: וְהַנָּחָשׁ הָיָה עָרוּם מִכֹּל חַיַּת הַשָּׂדֶה אֲשֶׁר עָשָׂה יְהוָה אֱלֹהִים וַיֹּאמֶר
אֶל־הָאִשָּׁה אַף כִּי־אָמַר אֱלֹהִים לֹא תֹאכְלוּ מִכֹּל עֵץ הַגָּן: "Now the serpent
was the shrewdest (*aw-room'*) of all the wild beasts that the Lord
God had made. He said to the woman, "Did God really say: You
shall not eat of any tree of the garden?"

11. This usage occurs sixteen times in the Hebrew Bible.
12. This usage occurs eleven times in the Hebrew Bible.

Notwithstanding the views of the biblical lexicographers, we believe their view that these are two distinct words to be misdirected in the case of the Adam and Eve story. Lexicographers see these as distinct words in part because they see them appearing in different chapters of Genesis. Yet let us not forget that the chapter and verse numbers found in all translations of the Hebrew bible only date to the thirteenth century.[13] A traditional Torah scroll (upon which these translations are based) has no chapter numbers nor verse numbers. Hence, the real context for these two verses is that they appear directly juxtaposed to each other. They are not in separate chapters or in separate stories. They are part of a single, unified narrative.

A second point that mitigates against the position of the biblical lexicographers is their own grammatical construct. They identify עָרֹום (pronounced *aw-rome'*) and עָרוּם (pronounced *aw-room'*) as distinct words, and they may well be correct. However, in our two verses, both are pronounced with the *aw-room'* construct. Thus, the words should have the same translation according to the lexicographers—crafty or clever—in both usages in this story. Nonetheless, translators consistently render the first (Genesis 2:25) as "naked" and the second (Genesis 3:1) as "clever" or "crafty."

How these terms are be used in the rest of the Bible is a worthwhile conversation, but it is clear to us that, in the context of these two verses, the words are intended to mean the same thing. What, then, is the rationale for the consistent use of "naked" for Adam and Eve and "crafty" for the serpent? We think the answer is sex.[14]

13. Archbishop Stephen Langton and Cardinal Hugo de Sancto Caro developed different schemas for systematic division of the Bible in the early thirteenth century. The modern chapter divisions are based on Archbishop Langton's system.

14. The Jewish sages repeatedly see and comment on the sexual aspects of the story. See, for example, Tosefta Sotah 4; Pesiqta Zutra, Bereshit 2; and Yalqut Shimoni, Bereishit 257:25. Of these, the Pesiqta Zutra is most explicit on this matter. It says that it is contextually obvious that Adam and Eve were as naked as the animals and that they are described as "naked" (Genesis 2:25) only because the serpent saw them engage in sexual intercourse. He consequently became aroused and desired Eve, which is why he, too, is described as "naked" in the next verse (Genesis 3:1).

It should be clear from the last few verses of chapter 2 that the focus of the story is sexual. Nonetheless, there seems to be a desire among translators to desexualize the story and the serpent's role in it. Thus, the serpent is described as "cunning" or "clever." The desire to desexualize biblical stories is not new and is one we often encounter as teachers. We will give but one example to illustrate the point, and this, too, comes from the Adam and Eve story.

After the creation of woman, Adam says:

> Then the man said,
> "This one at last
> Is bone of my bones
> And flesh of my flesh.
> This one shall be called Woman,
> For from man was she taken" (Genesis 2:23).

The great medieval French commentator Rabbi Shlomo ben Yitzhak learns from this verse that Adam had sexual relations with all the animals, basing his commentary on the Talmud:

> And Rabbi Elazar said: What is [the meaning of] that [which] is written: "This is now bone of my bones and flesh of my flesh" (Genesis 2:23)? [This] teaches that Adam had intercourse with each animal and beast [in his search for his mate], and his mind was not at ease, [in accordance with the verse: "And for Adam, there was not found a helpmate for him" (Genesis 2:20)], until he had intercourse with Eve" (Yevamot 63a).

Two of the most popular online translations of Rabbi Shlomo's commentary both desexualize his observations. The first, found on sefaria.org, translates his commentary as: "This teaches that Adam endeavoured [sic] to find a companion among all cattle and beasts, but found no satisfaction except in Eve." The second, found on chabad.org, states: "This teaches us that Adam came to all the animals and the beasts [in search of a mate], but he was not satisfied until he found Eve."

What is going on here? We are convinced that the desexualization of the story—calling the serpent "clever" instead of "naked" and avoiding the image of Adam committing bestiality—occurs because Genesis is often and sometimes exclusively only taught to children. How does one explain such things to children (or even to adults for that matter)? And so we are left, incorrectly in our view, with a crafty as opposed to a naked serpent.

Yet even an accurate translation presents its own problems. How could the serpent be "the most naked" of all the animals? Aren't all animals naked? For that matter, so were Adam and Eve at this point of the story! In truth, a more nuanced translation, one that fits the essence of the story and is particularly fitting for our times, would see the serpent as "lustful," as in, "Now the serpent was 'lustful' (or, more politely, the most sexually attuned) of all the wild beasts that the Lord God had made."

A horny snake? It is no more bizarre than the idea of one that walks and talks and clearly lusts after Eve. And this notion of a lustful snake is entirely consistent with the commonly held view that the serpent, whatever he may or may not have been, is a metaphor for sexuality run wild, something that is further reinforced by a second word in the Hebrew version of the story that modern readers might find problematic.

When God confronts Adam and Eve after they have eaten from the tree, He first turns to Adam for an explanation.[15] Adam avoids taking responsibility for his actions by blaming Eve and even God Himself: "The man said, 'The woman You put at my side—she gave me of the tree, and I ate'" (Genesis 3:12). God next turns to the woman and asks, "'What is this you have done!'" What does the woman reply? "'The serpent [הִשִּׁיאַנִי], and I ate" (Genesis 3:13).

The root letters of a Hebrew word we again left untranslated (ש, א, and נ) are understood by the biblical lexicographers to connote lending on interest or being a creditor.[16] Thus, we have a translation of this word and of this verse that conveys no sense of any sexual tension: "The serpent duped me, and I ate." Yet, in

---

15. Common culture holds the fruit to be an apple. Jewish sources reject this and maintain that it was either a fig or a grape.

16. This usage occurs fifteen times in the Hebrew Bible.

modern Hebrew, these same root letters also mean "to marry."[17]
A modern reader of the Hebrew could well see here an alternative
translation that highlights the true sexual nature of the story: "The
serpent married me, and I ate."

Talk about a sexual metaphor!

A third linguistic element in this story confirms that it is
about sexuality and jealousy, and possibly even adultery. Look at
the punishments God doles out in the aftermath of this forbidden
meal.

> To Adam He said, "Because you did as your wife said and
> ate of the tree about which I commanded you, 'You shall
> not eat of it,'
> Cursed be the ground because of you;
> By toil shall you eat of it
> All the days of your life:
> Thorns and thistles shall it sprout for you.
> But your food shall be the grasses of the field;
> By the sweat of your brow
> Shall you get bread to eat,
> Until you return to the ground—
> For from it you were taken.
> For dust you are,
> And to dust you shall return." (Genesis 3:17–19).

Harsh, but logical, and also consistent with what we learned as
children about Adam. Children are taught that Adam was a kind
and good-natured (almost benign) keeper of the garden. He was
first and foremost a farmer, as the verses tell us: "God said, 'See, I
give you every seed-bearing plant that is upon all the earth, and
every tree that has seed-bearing fruit; they shall be yours for food"
(Genesis 1:29). The Adam we now see as adults violates the one

---

17. The three-letter root of this word in modern Hebrew is *nun*-sin-*ayin*,
whereas the three-letter root in the biblical usage is *nun*-shin-*ayin*. In the Torah, which has no vowels at all, the letters *sin* and *shin* look the same. One
reading from the original Hebrew could thus see the words as having the same
root letters and could easily read "married" instead of "duped."

command given him and, in doing so, he gains new insights into the concepts of "good" and "bad." Farmer that he was in the garden, so, too, will he be outside the garden. And with his newfound knowledge of good and bad, he is expected to go out into the world and do good.

If this were not a story about sex, we would expect a similar punishment for Eve. We would, of course, be wrong. "And to the woman He said, 'I will make most severe your pangs in childbearing; in pain shall you bear children. Yet your urge shall be for your husband, and he shall rule over you'" (Genesis 3:16). Is this a suitable punishment for eating the forbidden fruit? No, it's not, but it is quite appropriate for one who engages in consensual sexual pairings without being mindful of the hurt she may cause others. Her liaison with the serpent was by her choice, even if the serpent did lust after her. The pain she caused Adam with her adulterous coupling was surely real, and this pain rebounds onto her as "pangs in childbearing."

As for the serpent, he is cursed more than any of the animals, but God adds one more element to his punishment:

> "I will put enmity
> Between you and the woman,
> And between your offspring and hers;
> They shall strike at your head,
> And you shall strike at their heel" (Genesis 3:15).

Again, if this story is not about sex, why the emphasis on the enmity between the serpent and the woman? If this were just a story about eating a forbidden fruit (in a literal sense), this enmity should have extended to Adam, too. That it doesn't underscores the sexuality of the story and the tryst between the serpent and Eve. The enduring nature of this enmity also serves to highlight the ongoing consequences for humanity of the sexuality the serpent unleashed upon the world.

There is a final literary aspect to this story worth mentioning. The serpent, the third member of this love triangle, walks and talks and acts like a man. Why is he not called a man, and why is he given no backstory as were Adam and Eve?

The second question is easier to answer. He is the villain—a terrible villain, actually—one whose lust and selfish pursuit of sexual gratification have a lasting impact on humanity. Quite simply, he is undeserving of a backstory.[18]

As for the first, "he is a snake" is a common idiom in English for one who appears nice and acts sincerely, but who in truth is a backstabber. The use of snake as a metaphor for treachery was used by the Roman poet Virgil, who referred to a *Latet anguis in herba*, that is, a poisonous snake concealed in tall grass. It was first recorded in English in 1696 as the title of a book by Charles Leslie with a most intimidating title: *The snake in the grass or, Satan transform'd to an angel of light, discovering the deep and unsuspected subtilty which is couched under the pretended simplicity, of many of the principal leaders of people call'd Quakers.*

The Adam and Eve story shows us that the snake metaphor is much, much older than this, and much more powerful, too. The same is true for unbridled sexuality. As this story teaches us, consensual but misguided sexuality frequently causes serious harm to intimate personal relationships.

While the Adam and Eve saga may have set the stage for all the stories of sexual tension that follow, the jealousy the serpent felt toward Adam as he lusted for Eve pales in comparison to that which exists between Rachel and Leah. Their story has a fairy-tale quality at the outset but, unlike fairy tales, not everyone lives happily ever after.

Jacob first meets Rachel when he flees his parents' household after receiving the blessing of the firstborn in a deceitful manner.

---

18. It should be noted that the serpent was not always a villainous figure in the cultures of the ancient Near East. For example, the Uraeus serpent protected gods and kings from danger, and because of his snake nature, the king was immune to snake venom and could cure others. Protective snake figurines are also found in Mesopotamia, including reliefs and amulets of two snakes entwined, a symbol later inherited in Greek culture as the healing symbol of Asclepius. See Hendel, "Nehushtan," 615.

53

(We will discuss this aspect of the Jacob narrative in the chapter on sibling rivalry.) It is an emotional first encounter.

> There before his eyes was a well in the open. Three flocks of sheep were lying there beside it, for the flocks were watered from that well. The stone on the mouth of the well was large. When all the flocks were gathered there, the stone would be rolled from the mouth of the well and the sheep watered; then the stone would be put back in its place on the mouth of the well. Jacob said to them, "My friends, where are you from?" And they said, "We are from Haran." He said to them, "Do you know Laban the son of Nahor?" And they said, "Yes, we do." He continued, "Is he well?" They answered, "Yes, he is; and there is his daughter Rachel, coming with the flock." He said, "It is still broad daylight, too early to round up the animals; water the flock and take them to pasture." But they said, "We cannot, until all the flocks are rounded up; then the stone is rolled off the mouth of the well and we water the sheep." While he was still speaking with them, Rachel came with her father's flock; for she was a shepherdess. And when Jacob saw Rachel, the daughter of his uncle Laban, and the flock of his uncle Laban, Jacob went up and rolled the stone off the mouth of the well, and watered the flock of his uncle Laban. Then Jacob kissed Rachel, and broke into tears (Genesis 29:2–11).

Rachel brings Jacob to her home to meet her family, who are also his family because his mother, Rebekah, is the sister of Rachel's father, Laban. Jacob is an industrious type and quickly goes to work for his uncle to earn his keep. Yet even more quickly, he falls deeply in love with Rachel. "Now Laban had two daughters; the name of the older one was Leah, and the name of the younger was Rachel. Leah had weak eyes; Rachel was shapely and beautiful. Jacob loved Rachel; so he answered, 'I will serve you seven years for your younger daughter Rachel'" (Genesis 29:16–18). Here we have the paradigmatic love story in Genesis. So great was Jacob's love for Rachel that the seven years he labored for the right to marry her "seemed to him but a few days because of his love for her" (Genesis 29:20). But all does not end well. Jacob is duped by his future father-in-law, and the veiled woman under the wedding canopy is not Rachel at all but her older sister Leah. Somehow, both during the wedding feast and in their nuptial bed that night, Jacob fails to notice the switch. Come morning, he does, and he is overcome with righteous anger: "When morning came, there was Leah! So he said to Laban, 'What is this you have done to me? I was in your service for Rachel! Why did you deceive me?'" (Genesis 29:25). Laban, ever quick with a scheme, justifies his actions and makes a counterproposal.

> Laban said, "It is not the practice in our place to marry off the younger before the older. Wait until the bridal week of this one is over and we will give you that one too, provided you serve me another seven years." Jacob did so; he waited out the bridal week of the one, and then he gave him his daughter Rachel as wife.—Laban had given his maidservant Bilhah to his daughter Rachel as her maid.—And Jacob cohabited with Rachel also; indeed, he loved Rachel more than Leah. And he served him another seven years (Genesis 29:26–30).

It is at this point in the story that jealousy truly erupts between the two sisters who, according to rabbinic tradition, were once so very close, but who now must vie with one another for their husband's attention and affection.

Not surprisingly, given his love-at-first-sight romance with Rachel and the deceit perpetrated upon him by Laban, Jacob hates Leah (Genesis 29:31).[19] She of course is jealous of her sister, Rachel. But Leah has the great good fortune of being incredibly fertile, and she bears Jacob four sons in quick succession.

> Leah conceived and bore a son, and named him Reuben; for she declared, "It means: 'The Lord has seen my afflic-tion'; it also means: 'Now my husband will love me.'" She conceived again and bore a son, and declared, "This is because the Lord heard that I was unloved and has given

---

19. It should be noted that the Hebrew in this verse is unequivocal. It states that Lead is hated. Many English translations soften the Hebrew and render the verse as "Leah was unloved."

me this one also"; so she named him Simeon. Again she
conceived and bore a son and declared, "This time my
husband will become attached to me, for I have borne
him three sons." Therefore he was named Levi. She conceived again and bore a son, and declared, "This time I
will praise the Lord." Therefore she named him Judah.
Then she stopped bearing (Genesis 29:32–35).

Now it is time for Rachel to be jealous: "When Rachel saw that she
had borne Jacob no children, she became envious of her sister; and
Rachel said to Jacob, 'Give me children, or I shall die'" (Genesis
30:1). Jacob, who understands the limits of his relationship with
his Maker, is annoyed by Rachel's demands and responds somewhat insensitively: "Can I take the place of God, who has denied
you fruit of the womb?" (Genesis 30:2). With no other option open
to her, Rachel gives Jacob her maidservant Bilhah as a concubine,
"that she may bear on my knees and that through her I too may
have children" (Genesis 30:3). The plan works, although why Jacob, who is already struggling to keep two women happy and who
certainly must have heard of the tumultuous times his grandparents experienced when they brought a third party into their marriage, would agree to this is something of a mystery.

How does Leah react to all this, especially after Bilhah gives
birth to two sons? "When Leah saw that she had stopped bearing, she took her maid Zilpah and gave her to Jacob as concubine"
(Genesis 30:9).

And on and on it goes, a seemingly unending sexual competition between two sisters (and perhaps even between their two
concubines) that the storyline does nothing to hide. Indeed, arguably the snarkiest verse in the entire Pentateuch is found in this
narrative. It so happened while Rachel was still struggling with
her infertility issues that Leah's oldest son Reuben "came upon
some mandrakes in the field and brought them to his mother"
(Genesis 30:14). In those times, mandrakes were thought to have
fertility-enhancing properties, so Rachel innocently asks her sister
if she would give her some. Leah's response is painful to read, even

today: "'Was it not enough for you to take away my husband, that you would also take my son's mandrakes?'" (Genesis 30:15).

The consensual nature of the various sexual encounters we find in Genesis seems obvious. Yet, we do not believe that the story of Rachel and Leah appears in Genesis because it focuses on consent. It is instead a story of jealousy and the disastrous impact jealousy can have on intimate and personal relationships. This is what makes the account of Jacob and his wives a fitting morality tale for our times.

We would like to discuss one more tale of jealousy and lust, and that is the attempted seduction of Joseph by the wife of Potiphar. Unlike the jealousy stories we have examined so far, which involve couples with already established relationships, this is a story of desire, of longing for what one does not yet have. It is also the most destructive of the jealousy stories in Genesis.

Upon his arrival in Egypt, Joseph is sold as a slave to Potiphar, who is "a courtier of Pharaoh and his chief steward" (Genesis 39:1). Joseph was hard working and industrious, so Potiphar "took a liking to Joseph. He made him his personal attendant and put him in charge of his household, placing in his hands all that he owned" (Genesis 39:4). It was clear to all that God was with Joseph. More importantly for Potiphar, "the Lord blessed his house for Joseph's sake, so that the blessing of the Lord was upon everything that he owned, in the house and outside" (Genesis 39:5).

Things seemed to be going well for Joseph, at least as well as they could for a Hebrew enslaved in Egypt. His master trusted him implicitly and left him in charge of all his affairs. There was only one small problem. As the verse states, "Joseph was well built and handsome" (Genesis 39:6).

This is an odd interruption to the story. In modern America, research has shown that good looks do in fact contribute to one's success and advancement in the workplace, however unfair this may seem.[20] The ancient Egyptians were also known to be very particular about cleanliness and personal appearance, so much so that people who were poorly groomed were considered inferior.

20. See, for example, "Your Looks."

By dint of being a slave, Joseph would automatically have been assumed inferior to the Egyptians he served. Why, then, would they, or the story for that matter, be so interested in Joseph's physical appearance? Because Potiphar's wife, who remains nameless throughout this tale, is very, very interested in Joseph's looks.[21] More to the point, she lusts after the well-built and handsome Joseph: "After a time, his master's wife cast her eyes upon Joseph and said, 'Lie with me'" (Genesis 39:7).

At this point, the story takes an interesting turn. In contrast to the many other characters in Genesis who engage in consensual sex with little or no thought given to the consequences of their actions, Joseph does consider the aftermath of such an act. But why? Egypt is like the 1960s culture of the ancient world, a place in which free love and sex was seemingly everywhere.[22] Moreover, it is his master's wife who wants to sleep with him. How can he—how dare he—refuse? Here's why.

> But he refused. He said to his master's wife, "Look, with me here, my master gives no thought to anything in this house, and all that he owns he has placed in my hands. He wields no more authority in this house than I, and he has withheld nothing from me except yourself, since you are his wife. How then could I do this most wicked thing, and sin before God?" (Genesis 39:8–9).

21. It isn't until the medieval *Sefer HaYashar* that Potiphar's wife is given the Arabic name Zuleika, which means "fair, brilliant, lovely."

22. It is well known that the mythology of ancient Egypt relies heavily on sexual themes and is replete with tales of adultery, incest, and homosexuality (as evidenced by the stories of Seth and Horus). Masturbation also appears in Egyptian mythology, as seen in the creation myth that details how the first god (Atum or Ra) fathered the next generation of deities through masturbation. In short, the Egyptian gods were "earthy" enough to engage in sex, and it should come as no surprise that sexuality in ancient Egypt was open. Even necrophilia was widespread enough that, according to the writings of the Greek author Herodotus, the bodies of exceptionally beautiful women were not embalmed immediately after their deaths, but only after several days had passed, in order to prevent embalmers from having sex with the body. Scholarly research thus concludes, albeit in pejorative terms, that "widespread and gross immorality" flourished in ancient Egypt. See Reynolds, "Sex Morals," 21.

In taking this stand, Joseph worries about the thoughts and reactions of his master and overlooks those of his master's wife. She is undeterred. Day after day, she comes on to Joseph, and day after day, he says no (Genesis 39:10). But he cannot or will not avoid her, and she ultimately manipulates events so that she is alone with Joseph: "One such day, he came into the house to do his work. None of the household being there inside, she caught hold of him by his garment and said, 'Lie with me!' But he left his garment in her hand and got away and fled outside." (Genesis 39:11–12).

She is now angry, embarrassed, and wants revenge. For the other members of her household, she fabricates a story of attempted rape.

> When she saw that he had left it in her hand and had fled outside, she called out to her servants and said to them, "Look, he had to bring us a Hebrew to dally with us! This one came to lie with me; but I screamed loud. And when he heard me screaming at the top of my voice, he left his garment with me and got away and fled outside." (Genesis 39:13–15).

Yet, for her husband, she spun a new story with even more lucid details.

> She kept his garment beside her, until his master came home. Then she told him the same story, saying, "The Hebrew slave whom you brought into our house came to me to dally with me; but when I screamed at the top of my voice, he left his garment with me and fled outside." When his master heard the story that his wife told him, namely, "*Thus and so your slave did to me*," he was furious (Genesis 39:16, emphasis added).

Potiphar's wife is jealous for what she cannot have, namely, a sexual relationship with Joseph. Unable to obtain it, she sets out to destroy him. This explains the details of the rape she claims to have suffered at the hands of Joseph. "He did this to me," she claims, "and he put his hands here and here," all in the hope that her furious husband would have Joseph executed.

In the end, it seems that Potiphar does not truly believe his wife. Rather than have Joseph killed, he has him imprisoned—and not in an ordinary prison, but in the one where the king's prisoners are confined (Genesis 39:20). Joseph may yet live, but his life has been destroyed by the jealousy and lust of Potiphar's wife. Were it not for God's intervention, Joseph would surely have died in this prison instead of being elevated to the status of a prince in Egypt.

Exploitative Relationships

The final group of sexuality stories in Genesis introduces a new element that must be considered and analyzed: exploitation. It is not that these tales are bereft of lust and desire. They are present, but what we find is that one (and sometimes both) of the characters has more in mind than mere physical pleasure. He or she has ulterior motives driving the sexual union that marks a dramatic turning point in each story.

Judah and Tamar is one such story, and it doesn't have to be unlearned by adult readers of Genesis, because they certainly never learned it as children.

The story opens simply enough. Judah finds a wife, Tamar, for his oldest son Er. Er may have been a good husband (the text is silent on this point), but he was not a very good man: "Er, Judah's first-born, was displeasing to the Lord, and the Lord took his life" (Genesis 38:7). The prevailing custom of the time was that the widow of a man who died childless was expected to marry a brother of her deceased husband in a ceremony that came to be known as a levirate marriage. In this way, her first husband's name and legacy would carry on through the child fathered by his brother.

Here we encounter sexual exploitation for the first but certainly not the last time in this story. Tamar is exploited.[23] She is treated like chattel. She may consent to this marriage, but consent was the only option available to her (Genesis 38:8).

---

23. Unstated in the text, but clearly present from the vantage of the present, is the exploitation of Zilpah, Bilah, and Hagar.

Her second husband, Onan, may have been a better person than his brother Er, but he was a much worse husband: "Onan, knowing that the seed would not count as his, let it go to waste whenever he joined with his brother's wife, so as not to provide offspring for his brother" (Genesis 38:9). This, too, was evil in the eyes of God, and Onan, like his brother before him, dies by the hand of God (Genesis 38:10).

It is understandable that Judah comes to view Tamar as cursed, believing her somehow responsible for the deaths of two of his sons. (He did not and could not know the evil they did in the eyes of God.) So he exploits her a second time. Publicly, he proclaims: "'Stay as a widow in your father's house until my son Shelah grows up,'" implying that she will marry his third son at that time. Privately, we see his true motivations, for the verse states: "for he thought, 'He too might die like his brothers'" (Genesis 38:11).

Tamar, now twice exploited, is a trapped woman. Sent to live in her father's house, there she must stay for, by prevailing custom, she is the presumptive wife of Shelah. Yet it is clear from the verses that Judah will not allow her to marry another of his sons. What is she to do? She opts to turn the tables on her father-in-law and exploit him to regain control of her life.

The turn this tale now takes is complicated, and even the most cursory reading of it shows why children never learn this story.

> A long time afterward, Shua's daughter, the wife of Judah, died.[24] When his period of mourning was over, Judah went up to Timnah to his sheepshearers, together with his friend Hirah the Adullamite. And Tamar was told, "Your father-in-law is coming up to Timnah for the sheepshearing." So she took off her widow's garb, covered her face with a veil, and, wrapping herself up, sat down at the entrance to Enaim, which is on the road to Timnah; for she saw that Shelah was grown up, yet she had not been given to him as wife. When Judah saw her, he took her for a harlot; for she had covered her face. So

24. This is an excellent example of the common practice of "foreshadowing" in the Bible. These two sentences note that Judah's wife died, Judah properly mourned her, and implied that he was lonely.

he turned aside to her by the road and said, "Here, let me sleep with you"—for he did not know that she was his daughter-in-law. "What," she asked, "will you pay for sleeping with me?" He replied, "I will send a kid from my flock." But she said, "You must leave a pledge until you have sent it." And he said, "What pledge shall I give you?" She replied, "Your seal and cord, and the staff which you carry." So he gave them to her and slept with her, and she conceived by him. Then she went on her way. She took off her veil and again put on her widow's garb. Judah sent the kid by his friend the Adullamite, to redeem the pledge from the woman; but he could not find her. He inquired of the people of that town, "Where is the cult prostitute, the one at Enaim, by the road?" But they said, "There has been no prostitute here." So he returned to Judah and said, "I could not find her; moreover, the townspeople said: There has been no prostitute here." Judah said, "Let her keep them, lest we become a laughingstock. I did send her this kid, but you did not find her" (Genesis 38:12–23).

Is there a better example of how Genesis portrays a society in which consent, not law, governs sexuality? Prostitution is a public business, done out in in the open. So common is it that women trade their wares on credit. So bereft of shame and embarrassment is it that Judah does nothing to hide his identity. The only potential problem is that his high standing as a businessman might be compromised if he cannot find the prostitute and pay off his debt!

Returning to Tamar's actions and motivations, she is the exploiter in this instance. She stalks Judah. She tempts him. She has sex with him and, by doing so, conceives and is thus liberated from the burden of bearing a son in her first husband's name (albeit by her father-in-law and not a brother-in-law).

But she is not free from consequences.

After her liaison with Judah, she returns to her father's home where, we can only assume, she hopes and prays and waits to see if her plan comes to fruition. It does, in the most literal sense, but her father-in-law does not share her joy. "About three months later, Judah was told, 'Your daughter-in-law Tamar has played the harlot;

in fact, she is with child by harlotry.' 'Bring her out,' said Judah, 'and let her be burned'" (Genesis 38:24).[25]

Brazen as she might have been in formulating and executing her plan, Tamar is far more subtle even as she faces execution: "As she was being brought out, she sent this message to her father-in-law, 'I am with child by the man to whom these belong.' And she added, 'Examine these: whose seal and cord and staff are these?'" (Genesis 38:25). Judah does and then publicly acknowledges the paternity of the child. He adds: "'She is more in the right than I, inasmuch as I did not give her to my son Shelah'" (Genesis 38:26).

It seems, then, that this tale of mutual sexual exploitation worked out fine. For his part, Judah believes he saves the life of his son Shelah by not allowing him to marry Tamar. She, too, seems to have fulfilled her obligations vis-à-vis her first husband and should now be free to carry on with her life. Yet these are mere speculations, as the story tells us little more other than the fact that Tamar gives birth to twins. Let us therefore speculate and fill in the blanks.

This story is placed in the Pentateuch immediately after the sale of Joseph. Many scholars see Judah's disgrace being underscored by the juxtaposition of these two episodes. He argues for the sale of Joseph and, seeing their father's grief over the loss of his most beloved son, the other brothers banish Judah from their midst. This notion is reinforced by the fact that there is no mention of Judah's brothers in this story of Tamar. Judah's public standing was subsequently lowered even more by his conduct toward Tamar and his confession of paternity.[26]

25. There is much discussion among biblical scholars regarding whether Judah actually had the authority to have Tamar burned alive. According to some, people imposed severe penalties for infidelity in those days in order to deter others from committing the same sin.

26. The fact that Judah regains his standing with his brothers when he offers to be taken into slavery in place of Benjamin (Genesis 44) does not negate the humiliation and public disgrace he experiences at the time of this incident with Tamar.

As for Tamar, she is never mentioned again.[27] Could she have gone on to live a normal life? Would anyone in that time really have married a twice-widowed woman who conceived children with her father-in-law? We doubt it.[28]

As cautionary tales go, this one is a doozy, but it pales in comparison to the story of Dinah and Shechem.

Their story is frequently referred to as "the rape of Dinah," which explains why it, too, is never taught to children. So accepted is this version of the tale that many artists over the years have depicted it in exquisite detail. ("The Rape of Dinah," painted in 1531 by Giuliano Bugiardini, is but one example.) Our reading of the verses in Genesis 34, however, will show that it is a story about sexual exploitation, not rape. To fully appreciate how this reading makes so much sense, a bit of backstory is in order.

Dinah is the only daughter in a family with twelve sons. It would not be surprising if the family, especially her brothers, were overly protective of her. The Jewish biblical tradition about her relates the following: After spending twenty years with Laban, Jacob, returns to Canaan along with his wives and children. Yet the verse which details this journey mentions "his two wives, his two maidservants, and his eleven sons" (Genesis 32:23). Where is Dinah? Her father Jacob hid her away in a box, fearful that when they would inevitably encounter Esau on their journey home, he would see her and wish to take her as one of his wives.[29]

---

27. Although Tamar is not mentioned again, one of her sons is. David and his dynasty were descendants of Perez.

28. Proof of this can be gleaned from the Bible itself. Widows are deemed by God to need special protective care after the deaths of their husbands and are thus grouped together with the fatherless, poor, and resident alien as requiring God's protective care (Deuteronomy 24:17). Indeed, following the death of her husband, a widow's best hope for security would be her son's ability to provide for her. The loss of a son was thus an even greater tragedy for a widow, a fact underscored by the stories of miracles done for widows to prevent or restore the loss of their sons so the family can survive (1 Kings 17:17–24; 2 Kings 4:1–7). For a more detailed discussion, see Branch, "Biblical Views."

29. Esau already has two Canaanite wives—Adah, the daughter of Elon the Hittite, and Oholibamah, the daughter of Anah, daughter of Zibeon the Hivite—and a third, Basemath, daughter of Ishmael, sister of Nebaioth (Genesis

Is it any wonder, then, that Dinah feels boxed in, literally and figuratively? And is it not fitting that her story begins by stating: "Now Dinah, the daughter whom Leah had borne to Jacob, went out to visit the daughters of the land" (Genesis 34:1)?

As the story continues, we learn that she encounters Shechem, a prince of the land. What happens next depends on which translation of the Hebrew one relies on. The Hebrew is quite clear: "he took her and he lay with her" (Genesis 34:2). There is no doubt that they were sexually intimate. However, the next word in the verse, וַיְעַנֶּהָ, is translated in a variety of ways. Translations that favor the commonly held view that this is a story about rape render the word accordingly. Other translations prefer "and he humiliated her" (English Standard Version) or "and he humbled her" (Jewish Publication Society 1917 translation). This Hebrew term also connotes a sense of torment or mortification.

What is really going on?

If this is a story about sexual exploitation, which we believe it is, it is logical to think that Dinah sees Shechem as her ticket out of her suffocating family life. It is equally plausible that she flirts with him, that she wished to entice him, that she needs to exploit him. And this is what happens. The Hebrew "he took her" throughout Genesis has the sense not of forced, non-consensual sex, but of marriage. Shechem did not rape her. He married her and then consummated their marriage. Why, then, would the verse conclude with a term that implies humiliation, torment, or mortification? Because Shechem in turn needed to exploit Dinah. He was a prince. She was merely the daughter of a local shepherd. He was taken by her beauty and her alluring nature.[30] Nevertheless, he needed to be sure that Dinah understood their respective positions in their marriage.

36:2–3) It was common to take a wife from one's extended family, as Abraham does when he marries Sarah, who is his niece.

30. This is supported by the language of Genesis 34:3: "And his soul did cleave unto Dinah the daughter of Jacob, and he loved the damsel and spoke comfortingly unto the damsel" (Jewish Publication Society 1917 translation, which we have used here because it is truer to the Hebrew in this verse).

Additional details in the story indicate that it is about sexual exploitation rather than rape. For example, although he has already taken Dinah as his wife, Shechem asks his father to arrange a proper marriage ceremony (Genesis 34:4). Why? A public ceremony not only would be consistent with his position as prince, but it is also necessary because Dinah is an outsider. Would a prince go through all this effort to formalize his relationship to a shepherd girl he raped?

Consider also Jacob's response to the overtures of Hamor, the father of Shechem.

> And Hamor spoke with them, saying, "My son Shechem longs for your daughter. Please give her to him in marriage. Intermarry with us: give your daughters to us, and take our daughters for yourselves: You will dwell among us, and the land will be open before you; settle, move about, and acquire holdings in it." Then Shechem said to her father and brothers, "Do me this favor, and I will pay whatever you tell me. Ask of me a bride-price ever so high, as well as gifts, and I will pay what you tell me; only give me the maiden for a wife" (Genesis 34:8–12).

If this were truly a rape story, would Jacob ever have entertained such proposals? Of course not. Moreover, the real issue at hand is set forth clearly by Hamor in their exchange: "Intermarry with us." Intermarriage was the goal of both Dinah (who wanted to flee her family) and Shechem (whose soul was bound to Dinah according to Genesis 34:3), and for these reasons they sexually exploit each other.

Intermarriage also explains the differing reactions of Jacob and his sons, especially Simeon and Levi, to this entire episode. The story is quite expressive regarding the reactions of Dinah's brothers to her sexual liaison with Shechem: "The men were distressed and very angry, because he had committed an outrage in Israel by lying with Jacob's daughter—a thing not to be done" (Genesis 34:7).

Needless to say, rape is a thing not to be done, but this is about intermarriage, not rape. Given their heritage, the brothers' outrage is not misplaced. They are fiercely protective of Dinah and fiercely loyal to their tribe and its customs, first and foremost to their longstanding tradition of never marrying outsiders. Want proof? Abraham marries his niece Sarah and, in his advanced years, makes his devoted servant Eliezer take a solemn oath to find a wife for Isaac from among his family members back in Ur (Genesis 24:1–9). Isaac does so when he marries Rebekah, the daughter of his mother's brother. He in turn instructs his son Jacob to go to his mother's family to find a bride (Genesis 27:1–5), which Jacob does. Naturally, the brothers are unwilling to countenance intermarriage. It is quite simply a thing not to be done, and they were willing to go to great lengths, including deceit and outright lies, to make sure it is not done.

> [Simeon and Levi] said to [Hamor and Shechem], "We cannot do this thing, to give our sister to a man who is uncircumcised, for that is a disgrace among us. Only on this condition will we agree with you; that you will become like us in that every male among you is circumcised. Then we will give our daughters to you and take your daughters to ourselves; and we will dwell among you and become as one kindred. But if you will not listen to us and become circumcised, we will take our daughter and go" (Genesis 34:14–17).

Of course, this proposed arrangement greatly pleased Hamor and Shechem (Genesis 34:18). And of course, the brothers had no intention of honoring it. Worse still, two of them, Simeon and Levi, use it as an opportunity to demonstrate how far they will go to prevent intermarriage.

> On the third day, when they were in pain, Simeon and Levi, two of Jacob's sons, brothers of Dinah, took each his sword, came upon the city unmolested, and slew all the males. They put Hamor and his son Shechem to the sword, took Dinah out of Shechem's house, and went away. The other sons of Jacob came upon the slain and plundered the town, because their sister had been defiled. They seized their flocks and herds and asses, all that was inside the town and outside; all their wealth, all

their children, and their wives, all that was in the houses,
they took as captives and booty (Genesis 34:25-29).

Jacob is furious with his two sons: "'You have brought trouble on me, making me odious among the inhabitants of the land, the Canaanites and the Perizzites; my men are few in number, so that if they unite against me and attack me, I and my house will be destroyed'" (Genesis 34:30). It is not that Jacob is in favor of intermarriage. Far from it. He is simply willing to let Dinah leave the family rather than endanger the lives and well-being of the rest of them. Simeon and Levi, ideologues that they apparently were, disagree. Intermarriage is beyond the pale and must be prevented at any cost.

Lest one think that Jacob's stance mellows over the years, that he comes to see if not the wisdom at least the necessity of the actions of Simeon and Levi, just look at the blessing he gives these two on his deathbed.

> Simeon and Levi are a pair;
> Their weapons are tools of lawlessness.
> Let not my person be included in their council,
> Let not my being be counted in their assembly.
> For when angry they slay men,
> And when pleased they maim oxen.
> Cursed be their anger so fierce,
> And their wrath so relentless.
> I will divide them in Jacob,
> Scatter them in Israel (Genesis 49:5-7).

Could Dinah and Shechem have lived with their mutual sexual exploitation had Simeon and Levi not acted as they did? Who knows? Perhaps Dinah, once free of her family, would have left the man she used to escape. Perhaps Shechem, prince of his people, would have grown tired of the simple shepherd girl. What is certain is this: Where sex is casual, exploitation is always present, to the point of being commonplace. Consequences as violent as those in the story of Dinah and Shechem are rare but, as Genesis tells us again and again, there are always consequences—some predictable, some unforeseen—of sexual exploitation.

Sex is Complicated

For many Americans, sex today is casual and consensual. We have even heard young people compare it to food and their quest for new culinary experiences, as in: "I like trying new things. If it's good, great. If not, it's no big deal."

Sex in Genesis is anything but casual. It is complicated, and the complications arise from the preexisting relationships between the primary players. Aside from tales of sexual exploitation, the sexuality stories of Genesis are about relationships and how they are impacted by changes in the sexual status quo. Casual hookups, even when frequent or when they involve threesomes or any other sexual scenario, do not harm relationships because, by definition, hookups are devoid of relationship.[31] In contrast, the Genesis stories are all about relationships and how they unravel or are harmed by a change, albeit consensual, to the sexual dynamic. These stories are cautionary tales. They do not preach at us, nor do they come to pass judgment on the actions of the participants. Quite the contrary. These stories often present the decisions to change sexual conduct as rational and sensible. Yet, in the end, emotions trump rationality, and the consequences portrayed in these stories make Genesis an important read for our times.

---

31. We do not approve of "hook ups," and there is a large literature on why they are bad. Our point is that they are not relationships, rather than they are good. The extent to which frequent hookups impact one's self-esteem or are a reflection of one's existing levels of self-esteem is beyond the scope of our analysis.

CHAPTER 4

Marriage and Reproductive Issues

HAVING NOW SHOWN WHY Genesis is such an important morality tale dealing with sexual relations, let us turn our attention to the topic of marriage and reproductive issues.

Certain marriages throughout history have been considered iconic: Antony and Cleopatra.[1] Napoleon and Josephine.[2] Marie and Pierre.[3] Edward and Wallis.[4] For Americans of a certain age and generation, the iconic married couple is John and

1. They are arguably the most famous lovers in history. Marcus Antonius of Rome stood at the pinnacle of power, fighting to be the most powerful man in the known world; and Cleopatra VII Philopator was the queen of one ancient civilization, Egypt, and heir to the unmatched cultural achievements of another, Greece. Their love affair, their war together, their defeat and, finally, their suicides have been retold for centuries.

2. Even after they divorced, Napoleon insisted that Josephine retain the title Empress of France, saying "It is my will that she retain the rank and title of empress, and especially that she never doubt my sentiments, and that she ever hold me as her best and dearest friend."

3. The Curies' mixture of science and romance is epitomized by the fact that the blue wedding dress Marie wore when she married Pierre functioned as her lab coat thereafter.

4. Edward was the king of England, and Wallis Simpson was a divorced American socialite. The British government refused to accept her as queen, so he abdicated in 1936. Talk about true love.

Jacqueline Kennedy. The 1960s were a time of excitement and hope in America, and no one typified this more than the handsome, young president and his elegant wife. Yet there was a dark side to their marriage. President Kennedy was alleged to have said, "If I don't have sex every day, I get a headache," to anyone who would listen, from British Prime Minister Harold Macmillan to a lowly senatorial aide.[5] "Even in the pantheon of sexual narcissists drawn to politics, Kennedy's obsessive conquesting remains the gold standard for bad behavior."[6]

Kennedy was considered an outlier in his time in terms of his infidelities and his obsession with sex. Would he be seen in the same light today? It is hard to tell from current research on the topic of marriage. In a study conducted for the General Social Survey (GSS) in 2007, Tom W. Smith of the University of Chicago made the following observation:

> There are probably more scientifically worthless "facts" on extra-marital relations than on any other facet of human behavior. Popular magazines (e.g. *Redbook, Psychology Today, Cosmopolitan*), advice columnists (Dear Abby and Dr. Joyce Brothers), pop-sexologists (e.g., Morton Hunt and Shere Hite) have all conducted or reported on "studies" of extra-marital relations. These studies typically find extremely high levels of extra-marital activity . . . Hite for example reported that 70% of women married five or more years "are having sex outside of their marriage . . ." They also often claim that extra-marital relations have become much more common over time. Dr. Brothers . . ., for example, claims that 50% of married women now have sex outside of marriage, double the level of a generation ago.[7]

Smith's dismissive attitude toward these sources is obvious, and he goes on to argue that extramarital relations are less prevalent than pop and pseudoscientific accounts contend. He argues that

5. Stewart, "All the President's Women."
6. Stewart, "All the President's Women."
7. Smith, *American Sexual Behavior*, 8.

the best estimates are that about 3–4 percent of currently married people have a sexual partner besides their spouse in a given year, and that about 15 percent to 18 percent of ever-married people have had a sexual partner other than their spouse while married. Smith adds that extramarital relations are more common among younger adults, and he believes this to be largely a function of younger adults having been married for a shorter period of time. He notes that "some recently married people have difficulty adjusting from a premarital pattern of multiple sexual partners to a monogamous partnership and in general recent marriages are more likely to end in divorce than long-term marriages."[8]

One aspect of extramarital relations Smith does not address (nor do many other researchers) is the question of open marriage. The lack of data does not mean that it is not a real phenomenon. In 2017, the *New York Times Magazine* published an article entitled "Is an Open Marriage a Happier Marriage."[9] The article quotes a sex and couples therapist who speaks about the frequency with which she would encounter married couples whose ideas about fidelity were more lax than those she encountered at the outset of her career. She terms this phenomenon "the new monogamy," which she defines as follows: "The new monogamy is, baldly speaking, the recognition that, for an increasing number of couples, marital attachment involves a more fluid idea of connection to the primary partner than is true of the 'old monogamy.' Within the new notion of monogamy, each partner assumes that the other is, and will remain, the main attachment, but that outside attachments of one kind or another are allowed—as long as they don't threaten the primary connection."

Or consider what Franklin Veaux, co-author of the book *More Than Two: A Practical Guide to Ethical Polyamory*, wrote in an online blog: "Completely anecdotally, I would be surprised if the number of polyamorous people in the US was less than 4% of the population, but I would also be surprised if it was more than 9%. Add in swinging and other kinds of non-monogamy and my

8. Smith, *American Sexual Behavior*, 9.
9. Dominus, "Is an Open Marriage a Happier Marriage?"

guess would be perhaps around 12% or so."[10] We think the stronger anecdotal evidence is the number of how-to pieces one can find online with the quickest of Google searches, such as "7 Ways to Have an Open Relationship When You're Married," "Your Complete Guide to Making an Open Relationship Work," and "Open Marriages Are a Lot More Functional Than You Think."[11]

With the exception of divorce (and it is worth noting that divorce is absent in all these stories), all of these marital issues are part of the Genesis narrative. While the marriages we examined in the last chapter may not have been as open as those that exist today, the polyamorous nature of the Jewish patriarchal families had serious and lasting impacts on those involved. So, too, with Adam and Eve. They may have started their relationship in Eden but, as is clear from their story, their marriage was no paradise, especially in the aftermath of adultery and jealousy. There is, however, one couple portrayed in Genesis as committed to a monogamous relationship: Isaac and Rebekah. Despite this, their marriage is as complicated and fraught as those of the other patriarchs. Let us see why.

Their story opens three years after Abraham's attempt to sacrifice his son Isaac, an event that is immediately followed by the death of Isaac's beloved mother Sarah.[12] The text is silent on the aftermath of these traumatic events, although traditional rabbinic sources portray Isaac as still mourning his mother.[13] At this point, Abraham turns to his trusted servant Eliezer and asks him to take a binding oath "that you will not take a wife for my son from the daughters of the Canaanites among whom I dwell" (Genesis 24:3).

True to his word, Eliezer departs for the land of Abraham's birth, and upon arriving there, prays to the God of his master.

> And he said, "O Lord, God of my master Abraham, grant me good fortune this day, and deal graciously with

10. Sibi, "How Many Married Couples Have an Open Relationship?"

11. Lankford, "7 Ways"; Jalili, "Your Complete Guide"; and Patel, "Open Marriages."

12. See Genesis 23:1.

13. See Genesis 24:67 and the commentaries thereupon.

> my master Abraham: Here I stand by the spring as the
> daughters of the townsmen come out to draw water; let
> the maiden to whom I say, 'Please, lower your jar that I
> may drink,' and who replies, 'Drink, and I will also water
> your camels'—let her be the one whom You have decreed
> for Your servant Isaac. Thereby shall I know that You have
> dealt graciously with my master" (Genesis 24:12–14).

The text goes on to tell us that Eliezer has scarcely finished speaking when Rebekah appears with her jar on her shoulder (Genesis 24:15). She is seemingly the answer to Eliezer's prayers, for she offers him water to drink and volunteers to water his camels as well (Genesis 24:18–20). All that remains is to ascertain her identity; when she declares that she is the daughter of Bethuel, who was the son of Milcah, the wife of Abraham's brother Nahor, he realizes tht his prayer has indeed been answered. As a sign of gratitude, Eliezer "bowed low in homage to the Lord" (Genesis 24:26).

To complete his mission, Eliezer goes to meet Rebekah's family. He explains why he has come and details both his plea to God and how Rebekah fulfills the conditions of his prayer. The young girl's family is convinced, as they declare: "'The matter was decreed by the Lord; we cannot speak to you bad or good'" (Genesis 24:50). Consistent with the customs of the time, Eliezer "brought out objects of silver and gold, and garments, and gave them to Rebekah; and he gave presents to her brother and her mother" (Genesis 24:53). All that is left is to secure the girl's consent. "They called Rebekah and said to her, 'Will you go with this man?' And she said, 'I will'" (Genesis 24:58).

The storybook quality to this tale continues. Eliezer and Rebekah depart for Canaan. When they arrive, they find Isaac walking in the fields, toward evening (Genesis 24:63).[14] Rebekah spies him and alights from her camel, greatly taken by her husband-to-be (Genesis 24:65). Their initial encounter concludes with Isaac bringing Rebekah "into the tent of his mother Sarah, and he took

---

14. The Hebrew of the verse suggests that he was not merely walking but praying or meditating.

Rebekah as his wife. Isaac loved her, and thus found comfort after his mother's death" (Genesis 24:67).

The obvious question is, what happened? Where do the complications and difficulties that are so evident later in their story come from? Certainly not from the type of sexual tension that confounded the marriages of the other patriarchal families. We know that Isaac, when faced with a famine and forced to relocate from Canaan, uses the same ploy as his father, claiming that his wife is his sister (Genesis 26:1–7). The storyline of Isaac and Rebekah, however, is significantly different in two respects. First, she is *not* taken by Abimelech, the king of Gerar, so there is no notion of a polyamorous relationship. Second, Isaac and Rebekah do not shy away from sexual activity in an attempt to mask their true relationship. To the contrary, "[w]hen some time had passed, Abimelech king of the Philistines, looking out of the window, saw Isaac fondling (מְצַחֵק) his wife Rebekah" (Genesis 26:8).[15]

So the question remains. The verses do not explicitly tell us what happens, but it does not take much reading between the lines to see the source of their marital tension. One factor is the couple's fertility issues. For twenty long years, they try without success to have children.[16] Whether out of his great love for Rebekah or whether he wishes to avoid the marital issues his parents had once they brought a third partner into their marriage bed, Isaac opts *not* to take a concubine. Instead, he "pleaded with the Lord on behalf of his wife, because she was barren" (Genesis 25:21).

In modern times, studies and anecdotal sources talk about the anger couples feel because of their inability to conceive and their jealousy toward friends and acquaintances who are able to have children. "Couples are three times more likely to divorce . . . The impact of the hormones often leads women to have harder time moderating feelings, and feeling out of control is compounded

---

15. The Hebrew word translated as "fondling" could have easily been rendered as "having intercourse," as that is the sense of the biblical usage of מְצַחֵק.

16. From Genesis 25:20, we know that Isaac is forty years old when he marries Rebekah. Verse 26 of this same chapter informs us that he is sixty when Rebekah gives birth to Esau and Jacob.

with an impact on sex drive that reduces the sexual relationship to mechanics."[17] Why would we think that Isaac and Rebekah did not experience similar feelings and emotions?

Then there is their seeming inability to communicate with one another. This, too, is an area of focus among modern marriage counselors and therapists. As one put it, "[m]arriage without communication, without exchange of thoughts, feelings, and emotions is unsustainable."[18] Indeed, some studies have found that communication problems are the most common factor that leads to divorce.[19]

The narrative of their lives makes clear that the lack of communication between Isaac and Rebekah causes much tension between them, and this all starts during Rebekah's pregnancy. That for which she hoped and prayed has come to pass, but hers is a difficult pregnancy: "the children struggled in her womb, and she said, 'If so, why do I exist?' She went to inquire of the Lord" (Genesis 25:22). God does provide her with an answer, one of profound importance and significance:

> And the Lord answered her,
> "Two nations are in your womb,
> Two separate peoples shall issue from your body;
> One people shall be mightier than the other,
> And the older shall serve the younger" (Genesis 25:23).

Think about this answer for a moment. God Himself gave her an answer. He explained the cause of her difficulties and outlined the future not only of her children but of their descendants as well. And what does she do with this remarkable news? She keeps it to herself. Nowhere in their story do we see that Rebekah shares or even hints about it to Isaac.

We can speculate as to why they do not communicate. Perhaps it is the twenty-seven-year age difference between them; Isaac

---

17. From an anecdote related in Chris Bodenner, "When Infertility Threatens a Marriage."

18. Fisher, "3 Reasons."

19. "Poor Communication."

is forty when they marry and she, according to most opinions, is only thirteen years old at the time. Perhaps it is their different upbringings. Isaac is raised by God's emissaries, by two individuals who commit their lives to teaching others about the one true God. God Himself attests to the specialness of this household when He says of Abraham: "For I have singled him out, that he may instruct his children and his posterity to keep the way of the Lord by doing what is just and right" (Genesis 18:19). As for Rebekah, she grows up among idol worshippers in a family lacking in honesty and integrity, as is starkly demonstrated by the conduct of her brother Laban in his dealings with her son Jacob.

Regardless of the cause, these communication issues must have had an corrosive impact on their relationship, and we see evidence of this at arguably the most critical junction of their story: choosing an heir to receive the birthright and the mantle of leadership of their family, which presumably also means the responsibility for continuing the family's task of teaching the world of the one true God.

> When Isaac was old and his eyes were too dim to see, he called his older son Esau and said to him, "My son." He answered, "Here I am." And he said, "I am old now, and I do not know how soon I may die. Take your gear, your quiver and bow, and go out into the open and hunt me some game. Then prepare a dish for me such as I like, and bring it to me to eat, so that I may give you my innermost blessing before I die." Rebekah had been listening as Isaac spoke to his son Esau (Genesis 27:1–5).

Isaac does not consult Rebekah regarding this oh so very important decision. He does not even tell her about it. She is actually forced to eavesdrop in order to know what Isaac proposes to do. And because she is neither consulted nor informed, she has no opportunity to express her own opinions. Instead, she opts to act on her own, to deceive her husband, in order to bring about the fulfillment of God's prophecy which, of course, she never shared with her husband.

> When Esau had gone out into the open to hunt game to bring home, Rebekah said to her son Jacob, "I overheard your father speaking to your brother Esau, saying, 'Bring me some game and prepare a dish for me to eat, that I may bless you, with the Lord's approval, before I die.' Now, my son, listen carefully as I instruct you. Go to the flock and fetch me two choice kids, and I will make of them a dish for your father, such as he likes. Then take it to your father to eat, in order that he may bless you before he dies" (Genesis 27:5–10).

Understandably, Jacob is hesitant, even fearful, about joining in his mother's scheme. He shares his concern that, by doing so, he shall be cursed by his father instead of blessed (Genesis 27:12). Yet, Rebekah is steely in her determination to see her plan through: "But his mother said to him, 'Your curse, my son, be upon me! Just do as I say and go fetch them for me'" (Genesis 27:13).

We of course know the outcome of the story. Whatever sibling rivalry there already was between Esau and Jacob grows exponentially—a topic we will discuss at great length in the following chapter.

> When Esau heard his father's words, he burst into wild and bitter sobbing, and said to his father, "Bless me too, Father!" But he answered, "Your brother came with guile and took away your blessing." [Esau] said, "Was he, then, named Jacob that he might supplant me these two times? First he took away my birthright and now he has taken away my blessing!" And he added, "Have you not reserved a blessing for me?" Isaac answered, saying to Esau, "But I have made him master over you: I have given him all his brothers for servants, and sustained him with grain and wine. What, then, can I still do for you, my son?" And Esau said to his father, "Have you but one blessing, Father? Bless me too, Father!" And Esau wept aloud (Genesis 27:34–38).

Whatever doubts the reader may have about the depths of Esau's anger are swept aside by the internal dialogue recorded at the end of this incident: "Now Esau harbored a grudge against Jacob because of the blessing which his father had given him, and Esau said to himself, 'Let but the mourning period of my father come, and I will kill my brother Jacob" (Genesis 27:41).

A story that started on such a high concludes with a terrible low. Jacob must flee because of his brother's anger. He leaves to live with his uncle Laban, ostensibly to find a wife (Genesis 27:46–28:2), but Rebekah gives voice to the obvious. "'Now, my son, listen to me. Flee at once to Haran, to my brother Laban. Stay with him a while, until your brother's fury subsides—until your brother's anger against you subsides—and he forgets what you have done to him. Then I will fetch you from there. Let me not lose you both in one day!'" (Genesis 27:43–45). Sadly, Rebekah never sees her favored son again. She dies when Jacob is in exile, leaving Isaac alone, old and blind, bereft of the son he came to see, through God's intervention, as the rightful heir to the legacy begun by his father Abraham.[20]

What is Genesis trying to teach us with this story? Something that should be obvious to any modern reader. Marriage is hard. Love—true and deep love—may be a necessary first step, but it is not enough in and of itself to sustain a healthy relationship. A successful marriage requires attention and devotion to it by both parties. It demands that husband and wife work through and support each other during the difficult times, and perhaps nothing is more difficult for a couple who long for children than infertility. It insists on communication, honest and open. In short, it takes a lot for a marriage to thrive, even in the absence of the sexual issues that were present in so many of the other marriages portrayed in Genesis.

Perhaps the message of this story is readily apparent, but it is one worth repeating over and over, especially in our times. This is why the tale of Isaac and Rebekah is yet another example of how Genesis functions as a morality tale.

---

20. As Genesis 27:33 states: "Isaac was seized with very violent trembling. 'Who was it then,' he demanded, 'that hunted game and brought it to me? Moreover, I ate of it before you came, and I blessed him; now he must remain blessed!'"

CHAPTER 5

Sibling Rivalry

TELEVISION HAS GIVEN US some iconic sibling rivalries, such as Ross and Monica on *Friends* and Kelly and Bud from *Married . . . With Children*. Anyone who ever watched *The Brady Bunch* can relate to Jan's plaintive cry of "Marcia, Marcia, Marcia." And, of course, there is Bart Simpson, the bane of poor Lisa's existence. Yet sibling rivalries are not just the stuff of television fantasy. Parent-reported and observational studies put the number of conflicts among young siblings (seven and under) at three to seven an hour.[1] An hour! And it does not end as they grow up, because an older child will probably resent the younger for getting away with more, for being given more, and for being allowed to do more at an earlier age than the older child was permitted to do. The only solution seems to be better spacing between children, something along the lines of eight to ten years apart in age.[2]

Here is the simple truth. The more similarity there is between children—same sex, close in age, similar interests—the more sibling conflict over dominance and differentiation there is likely to be.[3] Anyone with children will attest to this, and so does the book of Genesis, over and over and over.

1. Dell'antonia, "Why Siblings Fight," SR6.
2. Pickhardt, "Sibling Conflict."
3. Pickhardt, "Sibling Conflict."

A Common Motif

That Genesis is replete with tales of sibling rivalry should come as no surprise. It is a theme found in many different cultures. In ancient Egypt, one finds the tale of Osiris, a primeval king, and his murder by his brother Set.[4] The Greeks wrote of Thyestes and Atreus, the sons of Pelops and Hippodamia, with their back-and-forth rivalry and the tragic consequences it spawned.[5] In Roman mythology, Romulus and his twin brother Remus were the founders of Rome. Their story is related by many authors, including Virgil, who claims their birth and adventures were fated to be.[6]

Incidences of sibling rivalry are not limited to ancient mythology. They are also present, for example, in a number of Shakespeare's plays. King Lear provokes rivalry among his three daughters by asking them to describe their love for him. In *The Taming of the Shrew*, sisters Kate and Bianca fight bitterly. In *Richard III*, the title character is at least partially motivated by rivalry with his brother, King Edward. In *As You Like It*, there is obvious sibling rivalry and antagonism between Orlando and Oliver and also between Duke Frederick and Duke Senior. Noteworthy, too, are the many adaptations of Sherlock Holmes and their depiction of his rivalry with his brother, Mycroft Holmes. Less subtle is John Steinbeck's *East of Eden*, in which the brothers Cal and Aron Trask are counterparts to Cain and Abel of the biblical story.

The literary motif of sibling rivalries echoes real life, and history contains some well-known feuding siblings. Shortly after Artaxerxes II became king of Persia in 404 BCE, he learned that his brother Cyrus was already planning to eliminate him. Ultimately, Cyrus amassed an army of 30,000 men and launched a full-on assault against Artaxerxes. In the midst of their definitive battle, they met face-to-face. Cyrus injured the king with his spear, but he sustained multiple dart wounds and died later that day. Likewise,

---

4. The story of Osiris is nicely summarized by McDermott, "Outstanding Story."

5. Details of this myth can be found at "Atreus & Thyestes."

6. See Garcia, "Romulus and Remus."

upon being crowned in 1553, the devoutly Catholic Queen Mary I sought to separate England from its Protestant infrastructure, something her half-sister, Elizabeth I, did not support. After a short-lived but unsuccessful rebellion against Mary, the queen accused Elizabeth of aiding its ringleaders and sentenced her to eight weeks imprisonment in the Tower of London. Or take the case of Al-Walid versus Suleiman: At its zenith, the Umayyad caliphate stood as one of history's largest empires, stretching from Spain to modern-day Iran. In 705, Al-Walid became its leader, a position he would not be allowed to pass on to his heir, because a precondition of his becoming caliph was that his brother, Suleiman, would rightfully assume the position after his death. Not surprisingly, Al-Walid tried to overturn this so that his son, 'Abd al-'Aziz, would succeed him. These efforts failed, and once Suleiman became caliph, he sought harsh vengeance upon all those who had supported his brother's child.

Incidents of jealous rivalries and internecine warfare are also evident in the animal kingdom. As reported by Peter Toohey in *Atlantic* magazine:

> The animal behaviorist Scott Forbes … describes how herpetologists, ornithologists, and mammalogists found that "infanticide—including siblicide—was a routine feature of family life in many species," most commonly seen in birds. Some birds lay two eggs "to insure against failure of the first egg to hatch. If both hatch, the second chick is redundant to the parents, and a potentially lethal competitor to the first-hatched progeny." The healthy, older chick often kills the younger to eliminate the competition, and some parents actually encourage siblicide when the death of the nest-mate doesn't naturally occur."[7]

Is this not what evolutionists expect and predict? Of course, the healthier, stronger offspring, presumably the firstborn, should prevail so that his (or her) genes are the ones to be passed on to the next generation.

7. Toohey, "Sibling Rivalry."

Significantly, as reported by Toohey, "Forbes thinks that there are discernible links between sibling rivalry in animals and humans."[8] Specifically, while Forbes thinks that such "extreme jealous reactions are not common in the human species," he notes that "the more modest forms of sibling rivalry that are ubiquitous in species with extensive parental care—the scrambles for food and begging competitions—resemble more closely the dynamics that occur in human families."[9]

The stories of sibling rivalry found in Genesis would seem consistent with Forbes's observations and would seem to reflect well-known tales from other cultures. Yet the portrayal of feuding siblings set forth in Genesis differs in one very important respect: the older sibling, with one exception, never triumphs. It is instead the younger brother who comes out on top, assuming that his rivalry with his brother or brothers does *not* result in his death!

Cain and Abel

It is ironic that the best known of the many sibling rivalry stories in Genesis is the only one which runs counter to the template of sibling interaction found throughout the book. Unlike every other sibling encounter depicted in Genesis, here it is the older sibling, Cain, who prevails.

But is triumph built on murder actually triumphant? More importantly, why must the foundational stories of Genesis include one that seems to teach the obvious, namely, that fratricide is a bad thing? What is really going on here, and what is the true enduring lesson to be gleaned from the story of Cain and Abel?

Let's start by examining the text itself.

> Now the man knew his wife Eve, and she conceived and bore Cain, saying, "I have gained a male child with the help of the Lord." She then bore his brother Abel. Abel became a keeper of sheep, and Cain became a tiller of the

8. Toohey, "Sibling Rivalry."
9. Toohey, "Sibling Rivalry."

soil. In the course of time, Cain brought an offering to the Lord from the fruit of the soil; and Abel, for his part, brought the choicest of the firstlings of his flock. The Lord paid heed to Abel and his offering, but to Cain and his offering He paid no heed. Cain was much distressed and his face fell. And the Lord said to Cain,

"Why are you distressed,

And why is your face fallen?

Surely, if you do right,

There is uplift.

But if you do not do right,

Sin crouches at the door;

Its urge is toward you,

Yet you can be its master."

Cain said to his brother Abel . . . and when they were in the field, Cain set upon his brother Abel and killed him (Genesis 4:1–8).

For the casual reader, the climax of the story—Abel's murder—overshadows important details that can help us make sense of this story. The first is the fact that it is Cain who conceives of bringing an offering to God, notwithstanding the fact that God does not accept his offering. This suggests that Cain may be the more spiritual of the brothers, a notion not often discussed, and one that makes Cain's subsequent actions all the more difficult to comprehend. And let's be clear. Understanding Cain's motives is key to uncovering the central lesson of this story because, ultimately, it is *his* story. Abel is merely a secondary character who is killed.

So what is it about Cain's offering that makes it less desirable? The text seems very clear on this topic. The originator, Cain, "brought an offering to the Lord from the fruit of the soil." Read the words carefully. Not from *his* soil, but from *the* soil, and not special or the choicest fruits, just fruit. In contrast, Abel, who seems to have been inspired by his brother's actions, goes the extra mile. He "brought the *choicest* of the firstlings of his flock."

There is a second linguistic hint worth noting, one which most English translations miss. The English rendering above states that "Abel, for his part, brought" an offering. The Hebrew corresponding to the phrase translated as "for his part" reads גַּם הוּא, which literally means "him too" or perhaps "himself also." Some see in this phrase a hint that Abel offers himself, as it were, as part of his offering to God, that he seeks a more personal and more intense connection with God than Cain does.

In the end, Abel invests a degree of thought and effort into his offering that is lacking in Cain's, and of course God notices this. This is why He "paid heed to Abel and his offering, but to Cain and his offering He paid no heed."[10]

For his part, Cain is "much distressed" that his offering was not accepted, but without obvious cause. God is not angry. God does not express disappointment with him. To the contrary, God offers words of encouragement to Cain in the poem:

> "Why are you distressed,
> And why is your face fallen?
> Surely, if you do right,
> There is uplift."

Yet Cain ignores these words intended to comfort him, just as he misses the prescient advice God offers him:

> "If you do not do right,
> Sin crouches at the door;
> Its urge is toward you."

What is God saying to Cain? Perhaps something along these lines: Your offering was a good start, but you can do better. You should strive to do better. But beware. You are angry, whether at yourself for not living up to your potential or at your brother for doing better than you with this. Regardless, do not let your anger fester and

---

10. The issue of why Cain underdelivers, so to speak, on this innovative idea is a fascinating question, but it does not directly impact our analysis of Cain's reactions to the rejection of his offering. Readers who wish to delve further into this should look at Fohrman, *Beast*. Abridged versions of his analyses can be found at Aish HaTorah (www.aish.com) in the site's Judaism 101 section (Exploring the Bible: Cain and Abel).

turn to jealousy, for jealousy is "the sin that crouches at the door," and it will lead you astray in everything you do.

We believe that this, and not the sin of fratricide, is the real morality aspect of this story. Sibling rivalries are a normal and unavoidable part of growing up. This is true even for the jealousy that can at times accompany such rivalries. Yet to allow the rivalry to fester and morph into anger and resentment is to invite sin in from the entrance of the door.

God tells Cain that "you can be its master." That he did not master it is the true point of the story. The story is included at the outset of Genesis to warn us to stop, pause, and contemplate. To step back from the raw and dangerous emotions that are about to engulf us. To be wary of the consequences of unchecked and bitter rivalries.

There are no other incidents of fratricide in Genesis—although, as we will see, it is given serious consideration by some. Why is this? Is it because the lesson of Cain and Abel resonates with the other siblings in Genesis? Or perhaps circumstances intervene to thwart their dark intentions? Answering these questions is the focus of the rest of this chapter.

Jacob and Esau

It is fair to say that the story of Jacob and Esau is the most complex and most nuanced of the sibling rivalries found in Genesis. In part, this is due to the sparse details Genesis conveys to us about their lives and their upbringing. But this is further complicated by the ambiguity of many of the verses themselves. Consider, for example, how the text describes Rebekah's pregnancy.

> Isaac was forty years old when he took to wife Rebekah, daughter of Bethuel the Aramean of Paddan-aram, sister of Laban the Aramean. Isaac pleaded with the Lord on behalf of his wife, because she was barren; and the Lord responded to his plea, and his wife Rebekah conceived. But the children struggled (ויתרוצצו) in her womb, and

she said, "If so, why do I exist?" She went to inquire of the
Lord (Genesis 25:20–22).

The Hebrew word ויתרוצצו is often translated in the context of this
verse as "struggled" because its literal meaning, running or moving quickly, is hard to reconcile with a woman's pregnancy. This
explains why the rabbinic tradition opts not to read this verse literally but instead understands it homiletically, as follows: "Whenever
she passed by the doors of Torah study, Jacob moved convulsively
in his efforts to come to birth, but whenever she passed by the
gate of a pagan temple, Esau moved convulsively in his efforts to
come to birth."[11] The rabbis offer yet another perspective on Rebekah's pregnancy. They imagine Jacob and Esau struggling with
one another and quarrelling as to how they should divide the two
worlds—the physical and the spiritual—as their inheritance.[12]

This rabbinic tradition notwithstanding, it is possible that the
obscure wording, ויתרוצצו, is meant to teach us something much
more basic. Maybe the rivalry between Jacob and Esau just *is*, that
it is akin to those animal rivalries that occur in nature, as described
by Forbes at the outset of this chapter. If so, this story would simply
reinforce the notion that sibling rivalries are a part of life and of
human experience that must be dealt with.

Yes, sibling rivalries have occurred and continue to occur
throughout history, and if the rivalry of Jacob and Esau were
merely that, merely one of life's regular occurrences, we do not
believe Genesis would have gone into such depth about their story.
Instead, it strikes us that there is more in play here. This is why we
believe there are two ways to parse their story and why we believe
a careful reading of the text will show this to be true.

Returning to the narrative itself, the verses tell us very little
about the upbringing of Jacob and Esau.

11. Genesis Rabbah 63:6.

12. Midrash Aggadah, Genesis 25:22:2. The implication of such an approach is that this is more than a mere story of brothers fighting for their parents' love and for tribal leadership. Rather, it is one of competing worldviews,
of competing ideologies and visions of right and wrong.

When her time to give birth was at hand, there were twins in her womb. The first one emerged red, like a hairy mantle all over; so they named him Esau. Then his brother emerged, holding on to the heel of Esau; so they named him Jacob. Isaac was sixty years old when they were born. When the boys grew up, Esau became a skillful hunter, a man of the outdoors; but Jacob was a mild man who stayed in camp (Genesis 25:24–27).

One fact, however, is clear: "Isaac favored Esau because he had a taste for game; but Rebekah favored Jacob" (Genesis 25:28). Parents showing favoritism? Not surprising, at least according to a recent study published in the *Journal of Marriage and Family* showing that 70 percent of mothers who participated in the survey admitted to having a favorite child.[13] And the impact of such favoritism? According to Karl Pillemer, PhD, director of the Cornell Institute for Translational Research on Aging and one of the authors of the study, "It doesn't matter whether you're the chosen child or not, the perception of unequal treatment has damaging effects for all siblings. The less favored kids may have ill will toward their mother or preferred sibling, and being the favored child brings resentment from one's siblings and the added weight of greater parental expectations."[14]

It is possible that this single factor—parental favoritism— fuels the competition between Esau and Jacob. Perhaps what we have here is some version of Freud's Oedipus complex. Perhaps the jealousy and anger Esau feels for Jacob is merely a reflection of a desire for his mother's affections. He may have been his father's favored son, but perhaps, at his core, Esau longs to be his mother's favorite son, too.

And Jacob? Who knows what resentments he harbored? How can we gauge the sense of inferiority Jacob may have felt in the presence of his older brother, the one who seemingly possessed the skills needed to be successful as a shepherd and their father's ultimate heir?

13. The study is cited in Vining, "Long Term Effects."
14. Quoted in Bryner, "Mom's Favoritism."

Is parental favoritism a factor in the rivalry of Jacob and Esau?[15] Most probably, but we dare not underestimate the financial and leadership issues that also underlie their conflict. The storyline in Genesis makes clear the financial stakes of this rivalry very early on.

> Once when Jacob was cooking a stew, Esau came in from the open, famished. And Esau said to Jacob, "Give me some of that red stuff to gulp down, for I am famished"—which is why he was named Edom. Jacob said, "First sell me your birthright." And Esau said, "I am at the point of death, so of what use is my birthright to me?" But Jacob said, "Swear to me first." So he swore to him, and sold his birthright to Jacob (Genesis 25:29–33).

What is this birthright that Esau so casually spurns (Genesis 25:34)? It is the double portion of his father's estate. While the text gives no overt hints about their age when this transaction takes place, traditional sources tell us that the twins were fifteen years old.

Why is Jacob so determined to obtain the birthright? As is the case so often in this story, the text leaves us guessing. Is it the resentment he may feel towards his brother? Or perhaps he understands, even at a young age, that Esau is not emotionally or spiritually suited to carry on the mission of their parents and grandparents, to teach the world about the one true God.

As for Esau, is it immaturity that drives his disinterest in the birthright? Or is it his perception that this is not a real sale—after all, who would actually sell his birthright for a bowl of soup? The verses are not clear on this point but, as an adult, Esau recalls this episode with great bitterness. After he discovers that Jacob tricked their father into giving him the blessing due the firstborn, Esau bitterly explains: "'Was he, then, named Jacob that he might supplant me these two times? First he took away my birthright and now he has taken away my blessing!'" (Genesis 27:36).

---

15. Ironically and sadly, this lesson is lost upon Jacob, as we will discuss later in this chapter.

As we have already seen, Esau's frustration and anger over the financial loss he has just suffered are great, and the story highlights the depths of his anguish: "And Esau said to his father, 'Have you but one blessing, Father? Bless me, too, Father!' And Esau wept aloud" (Genesis 27:38).

Unlike Cain before him, Esau has real cause to hate his brother, and he seems undeterred by Cain's ultimate fate when he contemplates how to deal with his brother Jacob: "Now Esau harbored a grudge against Jacob because of the blessing which his father had given him, and Esau said to himself, 'Let but the mourning period of my father come, and I will kill my brother Jacob'" (Genesis 27:41).

Would Esau have actually killed Jacob? We will never know, for Rebekah, either by intuition or Divine intervention, uncovers Esau's plot and quickly tells her beloved Jacob to flee to Haran to her brother Laban (Genesis 27:42–45). Yet the damage is done, and their family is torn asunder. Jacob spends twenty-two years in exile living with his uncle Laban. He never sees his mother again, for she dies while he is gone. Jacob sees Esau only once upon his return from exile. The story describes a bittersweet reunion: "Esau ran to greet him. He embraced him and, falling on his neck, he kissed him; and they wept" (Genesis 33:4).

Despite the apparent clarity of this verse, there are sources who doubt Esau's sincerity based on a scribal anomaly. While the letters in a traditional Torah scroll are not punctuated, the Hebrew word for "he embraced him" has dots above each of its letters. Some see these dots as a sign that Esau did not embrace Jacob wholeheartedly, that he still carried a grudge after all these years.[16]

If Genesis is a book of morality tales, as we believe it is, what is the lesson to be derived from the story of Jacob and Esau and their bitter rivalry? Simply this: Esau assumes that his position as the elder brother automatically grants him certain leadership and financial privileges. Nonetheless, when it comes time to bestow those privileges upon one of his sons, Isaac choses Jacob. Is his

16. Sifrei Bamidbar 69.2.

choice based on merit? Personality? A sign from God himself?[17] The real reason is irrelevant. The story makes clear that Jacob was, in his father's eyes and in the eyes of God, the right person at the right time to take the reins of leadership from his father, and Esau's unwillingness or inability to accept this reality had consequences that reverberated for years to come.[18]

Joseph and His Brothers

As we have noted, Esau pays little heed to the lessons to be learned from the story of Cain and Abel. Why would he? That story occurred more than twenty generations earlier according to *Ethics of the Fathers* (which was written about 1800 years ago and which is part of the mishna). Jacob, however, saw first-hand the consequences of a heated sibling rivalry, and he had to understand that the favoritism shown to him and his brother by their parents contributed to the bitterness that existed between them. "Isaac favored Esau because he had a taste for game; but Rebekah favored Jacob" (Genesis 25:28). Why, then, would he make the same mistake as his parents and thereby help foster the intense rivalry that develops between Joseph and his brothers?

When Jacob flees to Haran at his mother's urging to escape Esau's wrath, one of the first people he meets there is his cousin Rachel, the younger daughter of his uncle Laban (Genesis 29:1–12). Jacob quickly and intensely falls in love with Rachel. Indeed, while she is only one of the four women Jacob ultimately marries, she is the love of his life, as evidenced by his attitude toward the seven years he labored for Laban for the right to marry her: "So

17. As hinted at in Genesis 27:33.

18. From a Jewish perspective, the rivalry between Jacob and Esau was not limited to their lifetimes. It is clear from the Talmud and other sources that the ancient Romans who destroyed the Second Temple were viewed by the rabbis as descendants of Esau. Moreover, these sources see the struggle between Rome and Jerusalem as one between competing worldviews. This is a fascinating topic, but we are interested in the motivations and outcomes of the struggles between siblings in Genesis. In other words, we have examined Jacob and Esau as individuals, not as metaphors for good and evil.

Jacob served seven years for Rachel, and they seemed to him but a few days because of his love for her" (Genesis 29:20).

After being barren for many years, Rachel finally conceives and bears a son, Joseph, for Jacob. A few years pass, and Jacob, at the command of God (Genesis 31:3), begins the long trek back to his father's home in Canaan. During the journey, Rachel conceives again but dies in childbirth. With her dying breath, she asks that the boy be named Ben-Oni, "the son of my sorrow" (Genesis 35:18). So deep is Jacob's grief that he cannot comply. He instead names the child Benjamin, a Hebrew name that could be linked to the fact that the child was born in the southern part of Canaan or to the fact he was born in his father's "old days."[19]

In the face of such loss, is it surprising that Jacob would treasure the sons of his beloved Rachel to the point of loving them more than his other sons, to the point of showing favoritism to them? No, it is not, and this is exactly what Jacob does. "Now Israel loved Joseph best of all his sons, for he was the child of his old age; and he had made him an ornamented tunic" (Genesis 37:3).[20] This tunic may be an "amazing technicolor dreamcoat," to use the words of Tim Rice. It may be crafted from wool or fine linen. It may even be a vest. The precise meaning of the Hebrew term is unclear, and there are many commentaries on it. But one thing is unmistakably evident to Joseph, as well as to Jacob's other sons. This garment is a visible sign that Jacob sees in Joseph the person destined to become the leader of all the brothers, both at home and in the field.

As for the brothers, they react just as one might expect: "And when his brothers saw that their father loved him more than any of his brothers, they hated him so that they could not speak a friendly word to him" (Genesis 37:4).

There is another factor at play, less obvious but of equal importance to the enmity created by Jacob's favoritism. Their father

---

19. These explanations are brought by Rabbi Shlomo ben Yitzhak, better known by the acronym Rashi, in his commentary on Genesis 35:18.

20. Why and when he is called Jacob and why and when he is called Israel is worth examining, but it is a topic beyond the scope of our analysis.

may forget recent history when he favors Joseph over his other sons, but it is quite likely that the brothers do not. They surely remember that their great-grandfather Abraham sent away all his other sons and bequeathed his material and spiritual estates solely to Isaac (Genesis 25:1–6). Their grandfather, Isaac, in turn gave everything over to their father, Jacob. Given Joseph's elevated standing in the eyes of their father, would the brothers have expected any other outcome in terms of their inheritance? Would they not have seen Joseph as more than a future ruler to lord over them, but as a real threat to their very futures?

The sources of tension between Joseph and his brothers do not end here. The story tells us that Joseph brought "bad reports" about the sons of Leah to their father, Jacob.[21] The text gives no detail about what was contained in these reports, but the fact that they are described as "bad" is quite telling.[22] And let us not forget Joseph's dreams and his brothers' reactions to them.

> Once Joseph had a dream which he told to his brothers; and they hated him even more. He said to them, "Hear this dream which I have dreamed: There we were binding sheaves in the field, when suddenly my sheaf stood up and remained upright; then your sheaves gathered around and bowed low to my sheaf." His brothers answered, "Do you mean to reign over us? Do you mean to rule over us?" And they hated him even more for his talk about his dreams. He dreamed another dream and told it to his brothers, saying, "Look, I have had another dream: And this time, the sun, the moon, and eleven stars were bowing down to me." And when he told it to his father and brothers, his father berated him. "What," he said to him, "is this dream you have dreamed? Are we to come, I and your mother and your brothers, and bow low to you to the ground?" So his brothers were wrought up

---

21. Rashi on Genesis 37:2.

22. One commentator, Rabbi Yitzhak ben Shlomo, famously posits that the "evil report" mentioned in 37:2 consisted of Joseph telling his father that his brothers used to eat flesh cut off from a living animal, that they treated the sons of the handmaids with contempt, calling them slaves, and that they were suspected of living in an immoral, promiscuous manner.

at him, and his father kept the matter in mind (Genesis 37:5–11).

Like their uncle before them, the brothers seem unmindful of the legacy of Cain and Abel. And so, when their father inexplicably sends Joseph, alone, out to where they are pasturing the flocks, they see an unexpected opportunity. "They saw him from afar, and before he came close to them they conspired to kill him. They said to one another, 'Here comes that dreamer! Come now, let us kill him and throw him into one of the pits; and we can say, "A savage beast devoured him." We shall see what comes of his dreams!'" (Genesis 37:18–20).

We have seen this before in Genesis, sibling rivalry about to result in fratricide. In the case of Cain, it actually comes to be. With Esau, circumstances—and a quick-thinking mother—keep it from happening. But here, with Joseph and his brothers, a third possibility presents itself when Reuben argues forcibly against fratricide: "But when Reuben heard it, he tried to save him from them. He said, 'Let us not take his life.' And Reuben went on, 'Shed no blood! Cast him into that pit out in the wilderness, but do not touch him yourselves'—intending to save him from them and restore him to his father" (Genesis 37:21–22).

Neither the story nor the lessons Genesis wishes to impart about sibling rivalries ends at this point. Joseph is pulled from the pit by Midianite traders and sold into slavery (Genesis 37:28). When he arrives in Egypt, Joseph is purchased by Potiphar, a courtier of Pharaoh and his chief steward (Genesis 37:36). Potiphar's wife attempts to seduce him. Joseph rebuffs her advances but ends up in prison for twelve years (Genesis 39:7–20). In prison, he interprets the dreams of Pharaoh's cupbearer and baker, who had been locked away for having given "offense to their lord the king of Egypt" (Genesis 40:1). Ultimately, when Pharaoh has dreams that neither the magicians of Egypt nor all its wise men could interpret (Genesis 41:8), Joseph is brought before the king and offers these interpretations of Pharaoh's dreams.

And Joseph said to Pharaoh, "Pharaoh's dreams are one and the same: God has told Pharaoh what He is about to do. The seven healthy cows are seven years, and the seven healthy ears are seven years; it is the same dream. The seven lean and ugly cows that followed are seven years, as are also the seven empty ears scorched by the east wind; they are seven years of famine. It is just as I have told Pharaoh: God has revealed to Pharaoh what He is about to do. Immediately ahead are seven years of great abundance in all the land of Egypt. After them will come seven years of famine, and all the abundance in the land of Egypt will be forgotten. As the land is ravaged by famine, no trace of the abundance will be left in the land because of the famine thereafter, for it will be very severe. As for Pharaoh having had the same dream twice, it means that the matter has been determined by God, and that God will soon carry it out (Genesis 41:25–32).

Joseph goes on to suggest to Pharaoh that he "'find a man of discernment and wisdom, and set him over the land of Egypt'" (Genesis 41:33). This idea resonates with Pharaoh, and he immediately appoints Joseph to the position: "And Pharaoh said to his courtiers, 'Could we find another like him, a man in whom is the spirit of God?'" (Genesis 41:38).

Joseph is thus positioned to lead Egypt through the years of plenty and the years of famine. It is during the latter that the brothers go down to Egypt seeking food, and it is then that Joseph recognizes them (Genesis 42:1–7). Rather than immediately reveal himself, Joseph manipulates circumstances and events to see whether his brothers have come to regret their role in his being sold into slavery. They do, even though they are unaware that Joseph hears and understands their confessions of remorse.

They said to one another, "Alas, we are being punished on account of our brother, because we looked on at his anguish, yet paid no heed as he pleaded with us. That is why this distress has come upon us." Then Reuben spoke up and said to them, "Did I not tell you, 'Do no wrong to the boy'? But you paid no heed. Now comes the reckoning for his blood." They did not know that Joseph

95

understood, for there was an interpreter between him
and them (Genesis 42:21–23).

After much drama, Joseph reveals himself to his brothers: "'I am
Joseph. Is my father still well?'" (Genesis 45:3). Is this to be the
one tale of sibling rivalry in Genesis that ends well? Not quite. The
brothers may well be remorseful, but they are skeptical that Joseph
could or would be so forgiving.

> Joseph said to his brothers, "I am Joseph. Is my father
> still well?" But his brothers could not answer him, so
> dumfounded were they on account of him. Then Joseph
> said to his brothers, "Come forward to me." And when
> they came forward, he said, "I am your brother Joseph,
> he whom you sold into Egypt. Now, do not be distressed
> or reproach yourselves because you sold me hither; it
> was to save life that God sent me ahead of you (Genesis
> 45:3–5).

Only after Joseph tearfully embraces his brother Benjamin, only
after he then kisses all his other brothers and weeps upon them,
can his brothers speak to him (Genesis 45:14–15). Jacob is brought
down to Egypt, where he has an understandably emotional reunion with Joseph, and Joseph goes on to care for the families of
his father and his brothers for many years—a wonderful lesson in
forgive and forget, except that the brothers do not forget, and they
do not truly believe that Joseph has forgiven them.

> When Joseph's brothers saw that their father was dead,
> they said, "What if Joseph still bears a grudge against us
> and pays us back for all the wrong that we did him!" So
> they sent this message to Joseph, "Before his death your
> father left this instruction: So shall you say to Joseph,
> 'Forgive, I urge you, the offense and guilt of your broth-
> ers who treated you so harshly.' Therefore, please forgive
> the offense of the servants of the God of your father."
> And Joseph was in tears as they spoke to him. His broth-
> ers went to him themselves, flung themselves before him,
> and said, "We are prepared to be your slaves" (Genesis
> 50:15–18).

Thus is the nature of the morality tales of Genesis. Stories of sibling rivalry never end well. There is death. There is exile. And even when neither is present, the family is fractured beyond repair, never to be fully healed. This is why Joseph weeps in the face of the fears of his brothers. Joseph, who has forgiven the unforgivable, who has supported all this extended family's needs, who, alone among his brothers, sees God's hand behind all that has befallen him, this same Joseph cannot truly restore real familial bonds with his brothers.[23]

Presumption of Privilege

The sibling rivalry stories in Genesis need to be read in the context of the larger societies in which they were taking place. In the world outside of Genesis, it was common that the firstborn automatically was made the head of the family and typically also acted as the priest and the one closest to the gods his family worshipped. The hierarchy of this other world was thus built upon a presumption of privilege and power.

---

23. While family unity is never fully restored in Joseph's lifetime, and indeed, his rivalry with Judah is a much-discussed theme in the books of the Prophets, God foresees the ultimate reunification of the two and of all the Jewish people, as prophesied by Ezekiel: "And you, O mortal, take a stick and write on it, "Of Judah and the Israelites associated with him"; and take another stick and write on it, 'Of Joseph—the stick of Ephraim—and all the House of Israel associated with him.' Bring them close to each other, so that they become one stick, joined together in your hand. And when any of your people ask you, 'Won't you tell us what these actions of yours mean?' answer them, 'Thus said the Lord GOD: I am going to take the stick of Joseph—which is in the hand of Ephraim—and of the tribes of Israel associated with him, and I will place the stick of Judah upon it and make them into one stick; they shall be joined in My hand.' You shall hold up before their eyes the sticks which you have inscribed, and you shall declare to them: Thus said the Lord GOD: I am going to take the Israelite people from among the nations they have gone to, and gather them from every quarter, and bring them to their own land. I will make them a single nation in the land, on the hills of Israel, and one king shall be king of them all. Never again shall they be two nations, and never again shall they be divided into two kingdoms" (Ezekiel 37:16–22).

The stories of sibling rivalry we have looked at in Genesis stand in sharp distinction to this model. In Genesis, we see intense jealousy between siblings, sometimes driven by a longing to connect to God or to a parent and at other times by seeking power and wealth. In each, it is the older brother or brothers who are jealous, something that would never occur in the non-Genesis world because the older sibling knows that, merely by dint of birth order, it is he who will lead the family or inherit the lion's share of his father's wealth.

The Genesis stories of sibling rivalry clearly come to teach us something very different. In matters of leadership and inheritance, there can be no presumption of privilege. There is instead the merit of the individuals vying for power. "The older will serve the younger" (Genesis 25:23), so alien outside of Genesis, is the paradigm for power and leadership in Genesis.

What of cases in which the older sibling seemingly possesses the skills and talents necessary to assume the mantle of leadership? Is this not the case for Esau, the "skillful hunter" and "man of the outdoors"? Would he not be a more logical choice to take charge of his father's many flocks and servants? After all, is not Jacob "a mild man who stayed in camp" (Genesis 25:27)? Despite all this, Esau is ultimately not deemed by his father or by God to be the right person at that time, as Genesis makes clear in 28:1-9.

It therefore seems reasonable to see in these sibling rivalry stories an implicit lesson in humility, that Genesis is stressing via these stories the notion that God chooses the weak and the downtrodden as opposed to the firstborn. This idea is consistent with that found in the Prophets: "A little one shall become a thousand, and a small one a strong nation" (Isaiah 60:22).

In the end, we cannot say for sure why God favors the younger in each of the sibling rivalries set forth in Genesis. The real reason why, from the perspective of Genesis, is unimportant, for God need not justify His decision nor explain His reasons.

In our tumultuous times, when advantages such as race, gender, and wealth, which formerly granted one power and influence, are no longer assurances of either, these tales of sibling rivalry can and ought to have special resonance. Only when the elder siblings (in a literal or figurative sense) grasp and accept these lessons—that privilege ought to be earned and not inherited—will our society avoid the disruptions and splintering suffered by the families whose tales Genesis tells us.

CHAPTER 6

Why a Book of Genesis?

THERE IS ONE LAST question to address, even though it has nothing at all to do with the themes in Genesis we have examined so far. We are not so sure that it is even related to the morality tale aspects we see evidenced throughout Genesis. It is, however, very much a twenty-first century question, and it involves belief in God.

Belief in God, it seems, is becoming a rarer commodity.

At first glance, this assertion does not appear to be true. When asked by Gallup in a June 2016 survey if they believed in God, 89 percent of Americans said they did.[1] When Gallup first asked this question of Americans back in 1944, 96 percent answered in the affirmative. When Gallup later modified the wording in 1976 and asked Americans about their belief in "God or a universal spirit," 94 to 96 percent responded in the affirmative through 1994. Since 2011, Gallup has asked both questions of random half-samples of Americans.[2] The results on both questions have been similar, which indicates that adding "universal spirit" into the mix does not significantly affect how Americans respond to the question.

---

1. Newport, "Most Americans."

2. Random sampling is a part of the sampling technique in which each sample has an equal probability of being chosen. A sample chosen randomly is meant to be an unbiased representation of the total population.

Since 2013, the percentage of people who believe in God or a universal spirit has been consistently in the upper 80-percent range.

Taken at face value, belief in God would seem strong among Americans, even in the twenty-first century. Yet it is worth looking a bit more closely at the numbers.

In April 2018, the Pew Research Center also reported that nearly nine out of ten Americans said they believed in God.[3] But these researchers probed more deeply into what the respondents were really saying, especially those professing not to believe in God. When respondents say they do not believe in God, what are they actually rejecting? Are they rejecting belief in any higher power or spiritual force in the universe? Or are they rejecting only a traditional idea of God as shared by Jews and Christians, perhaps recalling images of a bearded man in the sky? Conversely, when respondents say they do believe in God, what do they believe in: God as described in the Bible or some other spiritual force or Supreme Being?

For these reasons, the Pew Research Center went on to survey more than 4,700 US adults. Their findings? One-third of Americans say they do not believe in the "God of the Bible," but that they do believe there is some other higher power or spiritual force in the universe. A slim majority of Americans (56 percent) said they believe in God "as described in the Bible." And one in ten do not believe in any higher power or spiritual force.[4]

Wait. There's more.

The number of atheists in the US is still a matter of considerable debate. As we see from both Gallup and Pew, only about one in ten Americans report that they do not believe in God, and only about 3 percent identify as atheist. However, a new study suggests that the true number of atheists could be much larger, perhaps even ten times larger than previously estimated. William M. Gervais and Maxine B. Najle used a novel way to measure atheist identity.[5] Instead of asking about belief in God directly, they

3. "When Americans Say."
4. "When Americans Say."
5. Gervais and Najle, "How Many Atheists."

provided a list of seemingly innocuous statements and then asked: "How many of these statements are true of you?" Respondents in a control group were given a list of nine statements, such as "I own a dog" and "I am a vegetarian." The test group received all the same statements plus one that read, "I do not believe in God." The totals from the test group were then compared to those from the control group, allowing researchers to estimate the number of people who identify as atheists without requiring any of the respondents to directly state that they do not believe in God. The study concludes that roughly one quarter (26 percent) of Americans likely do not believe in God. In reporting on this study, Daniel Cox, a research fellow for polling and public opinion at the American Enterprise Institute, writes that "while this result is fairly stunning and not consistent with any published survey results, there is good reason to suspect that more direct measures significantly underestimate the number of atheists."[6]

Even if one is to question the results of this particular study, the Pew research data we have already cited further notes a trend that is quite relevant to our discussion, namely that, compared with older Americans, fewer young adults believe in an active, engaged God.

According to Pew, majorities in all adult age groups say they believe in God or some other higher power, ranging from 83 percent of those ages eighteen to twenty-nine to 96 percent of those ages fifty to sixty-four. Young adults, however, are far less likely than their older counterparts to say they believe in God as described in the Bible. Whereas roughly two-thirds of adults ages fifty and older say they believe in the biblical God, just 49 percent of those in their thirties and forties and just 43 percent of adults under thirty say the same. A similar share of adults ages eighteen to twenty-nine say they believe in another higher power (39 percent).

The survey also shows that, compared with older adults, those under age fifty generally view God as less powerful and less involved in earthly affairs than do older Americans. At the same time, however, young adults are somewhat more likely than their

6. Cox, "Way More Americans."

elders to say they believe that they personally have been punished by God or a higher power in the universe.

Clearly, then, the question of God's existence continues to be relevant in our times, and the issue of belief in one true God, the Creator of the heavens and the earth, goes to the core of why there is a need for the book of Genesis. As we have indicated, the other four books of the Pentateuch together establish both the general narrative of the Jews as God's chosen people and set forth in great detail the legal requirements incumbent upon God's chosen people.[7] Genesis contributes next to nothing (only three commandments, as we have already pointed out) to the legal framework of the Pentateuch. In fairness, it does give us the history of Judaism's patriarchs and matriarchs. But, from God's perspective, the Jewish narrative could have begun with Exodus, with something along these lines: "A family of believers in the one true God descended to Egypt in the face of a severe famine in Canaan and were subsequently enslaved and abused by Pharaoh and his subjects. God sent a redeemer, Moses, to liberate these Hebrews from there and to bring them to encounter God Himself at Mount Sinai."

Why, then, begin the Pentateuch with Genesis?

Of all the grandiose themes and questions one might consider when studying Genesis, the most compelling and perplexing are these: Why does God create human beings? What is our purpose on this earth? This is, after all, the overwhelming question that humans have dealt with throughout our existence. In simplest terms, humans want to know why we are here.

In truth, this question hounds people of faith because they tend generally to focus more on the whys of this world, as opposed to the hows and the whats. This latter approach is bluntly framed by the evolutionary biologist and atheist Richard Dawkins who, in his book *River out of Eden*, writes: "The universe that we observe has precisely the properties we should expect if there is, at bottom, no design, no purpose, no evil and no good, nothing but blind,

---

7. The notion of God's chosen people is worthy of its own book, and we will not delve into it here.

pitiless indifference."[8] In this view, there is no answer to our question. There is no reason why. We just are.

Judaism, of course, rejects this notion. Yet the answers it brings are both varied and complicated. The one we believe can and should resonate with our modern times is a universalistic view put forward most succinctly in the writings of the twelfth-century scholar and philosopher, Rabbi Moses ben Maimon, commonly known as Maimonides. He deals with the question of the purpose of humanity by essentially not dealing with it. His basic premise is that we and everything else in creation are a part of God's will. To question our reason for being is, in many ways, an attempt to understand God's will, which is not something we can realistically achieve. Maimonides addresses this problem in his *Guide for the Perplexed* as part of a broader discussion of the purpose of creation.

> We remain firm in our belief that the whole Universe was created in accordance with the will of God, and we do not inquire for any other cause or object. Just as we do not ask what is the purpose of God's existence, so we do not ask what was the object of His will, which is the cause of the existence of all things with their present properties, both those that have been created and those that will be created.[9]

For Maimonides, the general purpose of the creation is both unknowable and beyond the scope of insignificant humans. There is no way of knowing or ascertaining this; hence we should humbly accept that it was the will of God that He created the world and humankind. Any questions beyond this are not acceptable to even ask.

Yet, in the world view of Maimonides, one may certainly ask why Genesis is included in the Pentateuch. Here is how he answers this question:

> It is one of the fundamental principles of the Law that the Universe has been created ex nihilo, and that of the

8. Dawkins, *River*, 131–32.

9. *Guide for the Perplexed*, Part 3, 13:2 (trans. Friedlander, 1903).

human race, one individual being, Adam, was created. As the time that elapsed from Adam to Moshe was not more than two thousand five hundred years, people would have doubted the truth of that statement if no other information had been added, seeing that the human race was spread over all parts of the earth in different families and with different languages, very unlike the one to the other. In order to remove this doubt the Law gives the genealogy of the nations (Gen. v. and x.), and the manner how they branched off from a common root. It names those of them who were well known, and tells who their fathers were, how long and where they lived. It describes also the cause that led to the dispersion of men over all parts of the earth, and to the formation of their different languages, after they had lived for a long time in one place, and spoken one language (ibid. xi.), as would be natural for descendants of one person. The accounts of the flood (ibid. vi-viii) and of the destruction of Sodom and Gomorrah (ibid. xix), serve as an illustration of the doctrine that "Verily there is a reward for the righteous; verily He is a God that judges in the earth" (Ps. lviii. 12).[10]

In brief, for Maimonides and those who subscribe to his views, Genesis is included in the Pentateuch for several reasons. First, to establish for us and to remind us that there is only one God in heaven. Genesis further informs us that the one God in heaven is the God of all, and that all human beings are required to worship this same God who is the universal God of all humanity.

This is an answer that resonates as strongly today as in the twelfth century when Maimonides first formulated it. Yet his is not the only, or even the most subscribed-to answer in Judaism to the question of why Genesis is part of the Pentateuch. In fact, the countervailing opinion goes completely against the universalistic approach favored by Maimonides and offers a very particularistic solution to this conundrum.

In wrestling with the purpose of Genesis, this second perspective bores down on an even narrower question: why does the Pentateuch begin with the story of creation? After all, why would

10. *Guide for the Perplexed*, Part 3, 50:3 (trans. Friedlander, 1903).

the Pentateuch start anywhere but "in the beginning"? Yet propo-
nents of this perspective are making a very fundamental point,
namely, that the Pentateuch is not a history book. The Pentateuch
is not and does not intend, for example, to be a faithful diary of
the life of Abraham, nor does it intend to give us a day-by-day
accounting of the life of Moses. It sometimes spends paragraphs
and paragraphs describing all the minutiae of a particular event in
a given era only to suddenly skip over the next five hundred years
in one verse. We get a description of why Noah is chosen to build
an ark and save humanity, whereas we are given no indication of
why Abraham becomes the first Jew. The text relates the details of
something most readers would find trivial—Eliezer's journey to
bring Rebekah back to Canaan to marry Isaac—in more than sixty
verses. All of this prompts us to ask: where is this level of detail for
things we see as much more important, such as the discussion between Abraham and Isaac on their way to the sacrifice on Mount
Moriah, or Isaac's rationale for wanting to give Esau the blessing
instead of Jacob, or why Jacob so openly shows favoritism toward
Joseph?

The fact is that it is neither true nor obvious that the Pentateuch should open with "in the beginning." This is why a number
of Jewish commentaries suggest that the Pentateuch could have
and perhaps should have begun with the verse in Exodus 12:2:
"This month will be for you the head of the months, the first of
them, of the months of the year." The command to sanctify the new
moon set forth in this verse is the first commandment given to the
Jewish people. If the Pentateuch were merely a book of law, one
that sets forth the commandments the Jews are to follow, this verse
from Exodus should have been its starting point. Clearly, detailing
and conveying commandments to the Jewish people cannot be the
sole point of the Torah.

Why, then, does God's revealed word to humans begin with
Genesis generally and creation specifically? In this particularistic
approach, the Pentateuch begins with the creation saga not because
we have any overwhelming interest in knowing that God created
all of humanity, nor because we have any literary or linguistic or

historical or even moral interest in really knowing about the story of Adam and Eve (or the subsequent stories of Noah and of Abraham, Isaac, and Jacob). The rationale for beginning the Pentateuch with Genesis is only to establish a very basic fact: *God owns everything, and the God who owns everything gave the Jews the Land of Israel.*

Let us take this approach one step further. Were it not necessary to establish the fact that God owns everything, the Pentateuch would have skipped Genesis entirely and would have begun either with the exodus from Egypt or with the first commandment (to sanctify the new moon). Otherwise, there is no readily apparent reason for including the book of Genesis in the Pentateuch. The Pentateuch makes Genesis the first of its five books only to show, first, that the Jews have the right to go into the Land of Israel and, second, to establish that ultimately God gave this land to the Jews. In this particularistic understanding of Genesis, establishing the connection of the Jewish people with the land of Israel is the book's purpose.

Just as we saw the relevance for our times of Maimonides's universalistic understanding of the "why Genesis" question, so, too, do we see the relevance of this particularistic approach to the question. Of the myriad of seemingly intractable problems facing twenty-first century politicians, few seem more daunting than the Israeli-Palestinian conflict. We are not here to take sides on any of the proposed solutions to this conflict. We merely wish to point out that this particularistic understanding of Genesis undergirds the Israelis' claim to this specific piece of real estate. Beyond their centuries-long connection with the land, apart from the two Jewish Commonwealths that existed in its borders, Jews today point to this particularistic reading of the creation story as part of their claim to the land.

Many American Christians share this sentiment. Christians of various denominations have long been enamored of the Jewish return to Zion. The predecessors to modern evangelical Christian Zionists are well known: sixteenth-century British theologians and seventeenth-century Puritan Divines. In fact, the Puritan Divines were a subgroup of Puritans who arose:

out of the sixteenth-century Protestant Reformation emerged popular interest in the fate of the Jewish people and a new covenantal thinking that tied the destiny of gentile nations to Jewish settlement in Palestine. Protestant theologians, by reading the Hebrew and early Christian prophetic books 'literally' instead of allegorically, came to believe that ancient Israel had never enjoyed complete domination over the land to which they were promised, and that God would yet fulfill those promises with the physical descendants of Abraham.[11]

American interest in Palestine, whether it was among eighteenth-century American revolutionaries or nineteenth- and twentieth-century liberal Protestants, was chiefly theological. Yet this interest became embedded in American thought. For example, in a book published in 1816, Elias Boudinot, a former president of the Continental Congress, wondered whether "God had raised up these United States in these latter days, for the very purpose of accomplishing his will in bringing his beloved people to their own land."[12] By 1891, the conservative evangelical William E. Blackstone, whom Louis Brandeis called the "father of Zionism," could produce more than four hundred signatures from the circles of American political and social elites—Supreme Court justices, senators, congressmen, and business tycoons—to urge President Benjamin Harrison to become like Cyrus and facilitate the return of the Jewish people to their homeland.[13]

Among contemporary Christian Zionists, belief in the historical accuracy of the biblical narratives influenced public opinion and helped make the case for a Jewish state. Nevertheless, in the first two decades of Israeli history, the ties between Israeli and American Jews and fundamentalist Christians were few.[14] Israel's remarkable (some would say miraculous) victory in the Six-Day War of 1967 changed the dynamics of this relationship. As Israeli

11. Hummel, "What's So American."
12. Boudinot, *Star*, 297.
13. Hummel, "What's So American."
14. Goldman, *Zeal*, 270.

journalist Gershom Gorenberg noted: "The Six-Day War did more than create a new political and military map in the Middle East. It also changed the mythic map, in a piece of the world where myths have always bent reality."[15]

Why Genesis? Answering this question may not be part of the book's timeless morality tale, but it is a question that continues to resonate for the modern student of the Bible.

15. Quoted in Goldman, *Zeal*, 271.

Epilogue

IN THIS BOOK, WE have examined independently three important themes in Genesis, along with the corollary question of why there is a need for the book of Genesis in the Pentateuch. Upon final reflection, it is hard not to see the links between them. The modern data demonstrate that there is a declining belief in God, at least in the God of Genesis, especially among younger people. We would expect this to correspond to a declining belief in the legal structure set forth in the Pentateuch, and this seems to be manifest in the sexual mores of our modern times. With increasing frequency, individuals are constrained in their sexual behavior not by a legal construct, but by their own personal sense of right and wrong—if they feel constrain at all as they go in search of new, pleasurable experiences. In any case, they are too often not mindful of the consequences of their actions, and this, we believe, explains in part the marriage crisis we see in modern America. As the data have demonstrated, fewer and fewer people are actually getting married, and those that do so later in life often end up getting divorced. Pamela Druckerman's marriage may have survived her sexual adventure, but many others do not.

In the end, what prompted us to write this book is our sense that we are today living in a Genesis-like setting. We have shown throughout our analysis that Genesis does not come to legislate legal conduct in terms of interpersonal relations. It is instead a book dominated by stories of consenting adults: Abraham and Sarah consent to bringing a third partner into their marriage. Jacob and his wives consent to his bringing two concubines into their home.

Tamar willingly and knowingly initiates a sexual liaison with her father-in-law Judah. Even Dinah was seduced by and then wanted to remain in a relationship with Shechem. The only implied (but not explicitly stated) red line in Genesis in terms of sexual conduct is rape, as we discussed in our treatment of the Joseph narrative.

This is the trend we see in America today. Our society is increasingly about personal liberties, personal freedoms, and personal choices. Druckerman and her contemporaries are free to engage in threesomes and then write about them without stigma. Unmarried cohabitating partners no longer need to hide their status. Same gender marriage is the law of the land. What the #MeToo movement has demonstrated is that with consent, all is permitted.

Let us be clear. We do not oppose the law of the United States permitting any of these acts. Indeed, we support nearly all of them. We write this book to highlight the moral challenges of happily living in such a society. It is too easy to confuse "legal" with "proper" or "wise." Being happily married, raising a family, and so much more is complex in a society that has no limitations on sexuality other than consent.

Yet what seems to be missing in our times is abundantly present throughout Genesis, and that is the notion of consequences. Genesis does not come to prohibit. It comes to teach us and to remind us that there are always consequences to our actions, even those entered into freely and willingly. Sometimes these consequences are (or should be) obvious, such as the profound impact of bringing a third person into a marriage. Sometimes they are unforeseen, such as brothers killing an entire town over their sister's intermarriage.

Without doubt, the ever-expanding freedoms we enjoy in America have brought much good to many, if not most of us. Just because something has been consented to by all parties and is in no way illegal, however, does not mean that it is harmless. This is the deep and universal message of Genesis, one suited for secular and religious individuals alike. This is why, perhaps more than ever, Genesis needs to be studied and relearned in an adult manner as the morality tale it truly is.

Bibliography

"Atreus & Thyestes." *Mythics.* http://mythics.info/english/mythology/atreus_en.htm.

Bodenner, Chris. "When Infertility Threatens a Marriage." *Atlantic* (October 26, 2016). https://www.theatlantic.com/notes/2016/10/when-infertility-threatens-marriage/505436/.

Boudinot, Elias. *A Star in the West, or, A Humble Attempt to Discover the Long Lost Ten Tribes of Israel: Preparatory to Their Return to Their Beloved City, Jerusalem.* Trenton, NJ: D. Fenton, S. Hutchinson, and J. Dunham, n.d.

Branch, Robin Gallaher. "Biblical Views: Biblical Widows—Groveling Grannies or Teaching Tools?" *Biblical Archaeology Review* 39, no. 1 (January/ February 2013) 28.

Bryner, Jeanna. "Mom's Favoritism Stings, Even for Adults." *Live Science* (June 28, 2010). https://www.livescience.com/8385-mom-favoritism-stings-adults.html.

Cox, Daniel. "Way More Americans May Be Atheists Than We Thought." *FiveThirtyEight* (May 18, 2017). https://fivethirtyeight.com/features/way-more-americans-may-be-atheists-than-we-thought/.

Dawkins, Richard. *River Out of Eden: A Darwinian View of Life.* New York: Basic, 1995.

Dell'antonia, K. J. "Why Siblings Fight." *New York Times* (July 8, 2018) SR6.

Dominus, Susan. "Is an Open Marriage a Happier Marriage?" *New York Times Magazine* (May 11, 2017). https://www.nytimes.com/2017/05/11/magazine/is-an-open-marriage-a-happier-marriage.html.

Druckerman, Pamela. *Bringing Up Bébé: One American Mother Discovers the Wisdom of French Parenting.* New York: Penguin, 2012.

———. "Why I Let My Husband Have a Threesome." *Esquire* (June 16, 2015). https://www.esquire.com/lifestyle/sex/a35748/threesome-for-husband-personal-essay/.

Fisher, Mary. "3 Reasons Why a Lack of Communication in Marriages Can Be Detrimental." *Marriage* (November 21, 2018). https://www.marriage.com/advice/communication/3-reasons-why-a-lack-of-communication-in-marriage-can-be-detrimental/.

Fohrman, David. *The Beast that Crouches at the Door*. Baltimore, MD: HFBS, 2007.

Garcia, Brittany. "Romulus and Remus." *Ancient History Encyclopedia* (April 18, 2018). https://www.ancient.eu/Romulus_and_Remus/.

Gervais, William M., and Maxine B. Najle. "How Many Atheists Are There?" *Social Psychological and Personality Science* 9, no. 1 (2018) 3–10. https://doi.org/10.1177/1948550617707015.

Goldman, Shalom L. *Zeal for Zion*. Chapel Hill: University of North Carolina Press, 2014.

Hendel, R. S. "Nehushtan נחשתן." Pages 615–16 in *Dictionary of Deities and Demons in the Bible*. Edited by Karel van der Toorn, Bob Becking, and Pieter W. van der Horst. Leiden: Brill and Grand Rapids, MI: Eerdmans, 1999.

Hummel, Dan. "What's So American about Christian Zionism?" *Religion & Politics* (May 9, 2018). http://religionandpolitics.org/2018/05/09/whats-so-american-about-christian-zionism/.

Jalili, Candice. "Your Complete Guide to Making an Open Relationship Work." *The Cut* (January 1, 2018). https://www.thecut.com/article/open-relationship-how-to-guide.html.

Lankford, Loren. "7 Ways to Have an Open Relationship When You're Married." *YourTango* (December 22, 2017). https://www.yourtango.com/20085129/7-tips-beginning-open-relationship.

Lee, Virginia S. "Unlearning: A Critical Element in the Learning Process." *Essays on Teaching Excellence toward the Best in the Academy* 14, no. 2 (2002–2003) n.p. https://cft.vanderbilt.edu/wp-content/uploads/sites/59/vol14n02_unlearning.htm.

McDermott, Alicia. "The Outstanding Story of Osiris: His Myth, Symbols, and Significance in Ancient Egypt." *Ancient Origins* (February 24, 2019). https://www.ancient-origins.net/human-origins-religions/story-osiris-how-first-ruler-egypt-became-god-underworld-008953.

Newport, Frank. "Most Americans Still Believe in God." *Gallup* (June 29, 2016). https://news.gallup.com/poll/193271/americans-believe-god.aspx.

Patel, Arti. "Open Marriages Are a Lot More Functional Than You Think." *Global News* (June 11, 2017). https://globalnews.ca/news/3512078/do-open-marriages-work/.

Pickhardt, Carl E. "Sibling Conflict in Adolescence." *Psychology Today* (March 2, 2010). https://www.psychologytoday.com/us/blog/surviving-your-childs-adolescence/201003/sibling-conflict-in-adolescence.

"Poor Communication Is The #1 Reason Couples Split Up: Survey." *Huffington Post* (November 20, 2013). https://www.huffingtonpost.com/2013/11/20/divorce-causes-_n_4304466.html.

Reynolds, James Bronson. "Sex Morals and The Law in Ancient Egypt and Babylon." *Journal of the American Institute of Criminal Law and Criminology* 5, no. 1 (1915) 20–31.

Sibi, Atti. "How Many Married Couples Have an Open Relationship?" *Quora* (April 26, 2017). https://www.quora.com/How-many-married-couples-have-an-open-relationship.

Smith, Tom W. *American Sexual Behavior: Trends, Socio-Demographic Differences, and Risk Behavior.* GSS Topical Report 25. Chicago, IL: National Opinion Research Center, March 2006. http://gss.norc.org/Documents/reports/topical-reports/sextrendo42-13.pdf.

Stewart, Sara. "All the President's Women." *New York Post* (November 10, 2013). https://nypost.com/2013/11/10/all-the-presidents-women-3/.

Tanakh: A New Translation of the Holy Scriptures according to the Traditional Hebrew Text. Philadelphia: Jewish Publication Society, 1985.

Toohey, Peter. "Sibling Rivalry, A History." *Atlantic* (November 30, 2014). https://www.theatlantic.com/health/archive/2014/11/sibling-rivalry-a-history/382964/.

Twenge, Jean M., et al. "Changes in American Adults' Sexual Behavior and Attitudes, 1972–2012." *Archives of Sexual Behavior* 44, no. 8 (2015) 2273–2285. doi: 10.1007/s10508-015-0540-2.

Vining, Season. "Long Term Effects of Parental Favoritism." *Baton Rouge Parents* (March 1, 2018). https://www.brparents.com/article/long-term-effects-of-parental-favoritism.html.

"When Americans Say They Believe in God, What Do They Mean?" *Pew Research Center* (April 25, 2018). http://www.pewforum.org/2018/04/25/when-americans-say-they-believe-in-god-what-do-they-mean/.

"Your Looks and Your Job: Does Appearance Affect Advancement?" *Career Intelligence* (n.d.). http://career-intelligence.com/appearance-affect-advancement/.

Printed in Great Britain
by Amazon

60749965R00077